TEST YOUR
LOGIC

TEST YOUR
LOGIC

•

50 Puzzles in

Deductive Reasoning

---

by **GEORGE J. SUMMERS**

•

Dover Publications, Inc.

New York

Published in Canada by General Publishing Company, Ltd., 30 Lesmill Road, Don Mills, Toronto, Ontario.

Test Your Logic: 50 Puzzles in Deductive Reasoning is a new work, first published in 1972 by Dover Publications, Inc.

International Standard Book Number: 0-486-22877-0
Library of Congress Catalog Card Number: 75-188244

Manufactured in the United States of America
Dover Publications, Inc.
31 East 2nd Street
Mineola, N.Y. 11501

Contents

*An asterisk indicates a puzzle which requires
an elementary knowledge of algebra.*

Introduction

The puzzles in this book have been composed to resemble short "who done it" mysteries. Each puzzle contains a number of clues, and it is up to the reader, or "detective," to determine from these clues which of various solutions is correct (or, to continue the analogy, which of various suspects is the culprit). In some of the puzzles an actual criminal must be sought, but the greater part of them concern more-or-less innocent people, or numbers.

The general method for solving these puzzles is as follows: The question posed at the end of each puzzle states a condition that must be met by the solution. For example, "which kind of card—Ace, King, Queen, or Jack—is card number six?" stipulates "is card number six" as a condition. The clues also stipulate conditions, either explicit or implied, involving the various "suspects." What the "detective" must do is discover all the conditions, and then determine which one—and only one—"suspect" satisfies the condition stated in the question.

Of the fifty puzzles, forty require no special knowledge. Numbers are involved in some of these, but no knowledge of algebra is necessary. Ten puzzles require knowledge of simple high school algebra.

1

Ham Yesterday, Pork Today

When Adrian, Buford, and Carter eat out, each orders either ham or pork.

1. If Adrian orders ham, Buford orders pork.
2. Either Adrian or Carter orders ham, but not both.
3. Buford and Carter do not both order pork.

Who could have ordered ham yesterday, pork today?

2

Val, Lynn, and Chris

Val, Lynn, and Chris are related to each other, but not incestuously.

1. Among the three are Val's father, Lynn's only daughter, and Chris' sibling.
2. Chris' sibling is neither Val's father nor Lynn's daughter.

Which one is a different sex from the other two?

Hint: Pick someone to be Val's father and reason from there; if a contradiction arises, pick someone else.

4

3

The Hospital Staff

"The hospital staff consists of 16 doctors and nurses, including me. The following facts apply to the staff members; whether you include me or not does not make any difference. The staff consists of:

1. More nurses than doctors.
2. More male doctors than male nurses.
3. More male nurses than female nurses.
4. At least one female doctor."

What is the sex and occupation of the speaker?

HINT: Determine the one distribution of male nurses, female nurses, male doctors, and female doctors that does not contradict the statements.

5

4

The Woman Freeman Will Marry

Freeman knows five women: Ada, Bea, Cyd, Deb, and Eve.

1. The women are in two age brackets: three women are under 30 and two women are over 30.
2. Two women are teachers and the other three women are secretaries.
3. Ada and Cyd are in the same age bracket.
4. Deb and Eve are in different age brackets.
5. Bea and Eve have the same occupation.
6. Cyd and Deb have different occupations.
7. Of the five women, Freeman will marry the teacher over 30.

Whom will Freeman marry?

HINT: Determine the women who are under 30 and the women who are secretaries.

5

Six A's

$$\begin{array}{r} A\,A\,A \\ B\,B\,B \\ +\,C\,C\,C \\ \hline F\,G\,H\,I \end{array} \qquad \begin{array}{r} A\,A\,A \\ D\,D\,D \\ +\,E\,E\,E \\ \hline F\,G\,H\,I \end{array}$$

In the additions above, each letter represents a different digit.

Which digit does A represent?

HINT: Determine the sums $A + B + C$ and $A + D + E$.

Not Remarkably Rich

Annette, Bernice, and Claudia are three remarkable women, each having some remarkable characteristics.

1. Just two are remarkably intelligent, just two are remarkably beautiful, just two are remarkably artistic, and just two are remarkably rich.
2. Each has no more than three remarkable characteristics.
3. Of Annette it is true that:
   if she is remarkably intelligent, she is remarkably rich.
4. Of Bernice and Claudia it is true that:
   if she is remarkably beautiful, she is remarkably artistic.
5. Of Annette and Claudia it is true that:
   if she is remarkably rich, she is remarkably artistic.

Who is not remarkably rich?

Hint: Determine the women who are artistic.

7

The Tennis Player

Two women, Alice and Carol, and two men, Brian and David, are athletes. One is a swimmer, a second is a skater, a third is a gymnast, and a fourth is a tennis player. On a day they were seated around a square table:

1. The swimmer sat on Alice's left.
2. The gymnast sat across from Brian.
3. Carol and David sat next to each other.
4. A woman sat on the skater's left.

Who is the tennis player?

HINT: Determine by names the different ways it is possible to seat the four people. Then determine which athletic titles can be applied to the names without contradicting any statement.

8

The Round

Anthony, Bernard, and Charles played a round of card games, each game having exactly one winner.

1. The player who first won three games was to be the winner of the round.
2. No player won two games in succession.
3. Anthony was the first dealer, but not the last.
4. Bernard was the second dealer.
5. The players sat in fixed positions around a table with the player on the current dealer's left the next dealer.
6. When a player was the dealer for a game he did not win that game.

Who won the round?

HINT: Determine the number of games that were played and who won the last game.

9

Three D's

In the multiplication below, each letter represents a different digit.

$$
\begin{array}{r}
A \\
\times \quad C\,B \\
\hline
E\,D \\
G\,F \\
\hline
D\,D\,D
\end{array}
$$

Which one of the ten digits does D represent?

10

Lawyers' Testimony

Albert, Barney, and Curtis were questioned about the murder of Dwight. Evidence at the scene of the crime indicated a lawyer might have been implicated in Dwight's murder.

Each suspect, one of whom was the murderer, made two statements as follows:

ALBERT:
1. I am not a lawyer.
2. I did not kill Dwight.

BARNEY:
3. I am a lawyer.
4. But I did not kill Dwight.

CURTIS:
5. I am not a lawyer.
6. A lawyer killed Dwight.

The police subsequently discovered that:
I. Only two of the above statements were true.
II. Only one of the three suspects was not a lawyer.

Who killed Dwight?

HINT: Determine whether both statements [2] and [4] are true or just one of statements [2] and [4] is true.

11

Spot Orientation

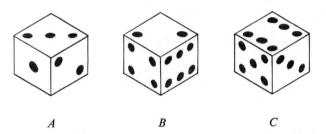

A   B   C

On a normal die, the sum of the numbers of spots on opposite faces is always seven; the three dice above are normal in that respect. However, two of the dice above are alike and one is different in respect to the orientation of their spots.

Which die—A, B, or C—is different?

Hint: Determine which faces have spots whose orientation can change; then determine whether these orientations are consistent in the dice.

13

12

Cora's Death

When Cora was killed, Anna and Beth were questioned by the police about the manner of her death by poison.

ANNA: If it was murder, Beth did it.
BETH: If it was not suicide, it was murder.

The police made the following assumptions:
1. If neither Anna nor Beth lied, it was an accident.
2. If either Anna or Beth lied, it was not an accident.

Subsequent developments revealed these assumptions were correct.

What was the manner of Cora's death: accident, suicide, or murder?

HINT: Determine the manner of Cora's death according to whether the women's statements are true or false; then determine the one assumption that can be applicable.

13

A Chair for Mr. Lancer

"Five married couples attended an anniversary dinner in honor of one of the husbands, Mr. Lancer. Chairs were arranged around an L-shaped table as shown in the diagram below.

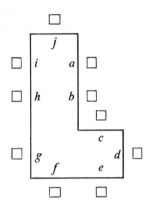

At the table:

1. Every man sat opposite a woman.
2. I sat in chair *a* opposite my husband.
3. No woman sat between two men.
4. Mr. Lancer sat between two women.

In which chair did Mr. Lancer sit?"

NOTE: "*Between two men (or women)*" *means to the left of one man (or woman) and to the right of another man (or woman), around the perimeter of the table.*

HINT: Determine the possible arrangements of men and women around the table without regard to specific chairs; then determine, beginning with the location of the speaker's chair, the possible arrangements with regard to specific chairs.

Decapitation of a Factor

$$
\begin{array}{r}
A\ B\ C\ D\ E\ F \\
\times \qquad\qquad M \\
\hline
B\ C\ D\ E\ F\ A
\end{array}
$$

In the multiplication above, each letter represents a different digit. Notice that if the "head" of the top factor falls to the rear it becomes the product.

Which one of the ten digits does M represent?

HINT: Choose values for *M* and *A* to determine the corresponding values for the remaining letters.

15

The Singleton

Dora, Lois, and Rose played a card game with 35 cards, consisting of 17 pairs and one singleton.

1. Dora dealt one card to Lois, then one card to Rose, then one card to herself, and repeated this order until all the cards were dealt.
2. After the pairs in each hand were removed, at least one card remained in each hand; the number of cards in the three hands totaled 9.
3. Of the remaining cards, Lois' and Dora's hands together formed the most pairs, and Rose's and Dora's hands together formed the least pairs.

Who was dealt the singleton?

HINT: Determine the number of cards dealt to each player and the number of pairs formed by each two hands.

16

The Sisters

Agnes, Betsy, Cindy, and Delia had just finished eating and drinking at their coffee break and were paying their checks.

1. Two women, each of whose coins totaled 60 cents, had the same number of silver coins; no denomination of coin was held by both women.
2. Two women, each of whose coins totaled 75 cents, had the same number of silver coins; no denomination of coin was held by both women.
3. Agnes' check was for 10 cents, Betsy's check was for 20 cents, Cindy's check was for 45 cents, and Delia's check was for 55 cents.
4. Each woman paid the exact amount of her check.
5. Two women, who were sisters, had the same number of coins left after paying their checks.

Which two women were sisters?

Note: *"Silver coins" may be nickels, dimes, quarters, or half dollars.*

Hint: First determine the four coin holdings, then determine who must have held each holding.

1𝟕

The Second Tournament

Alan, Bart, Clay, Dick, and Earl each played in two tennis tournaments.

1. In each tournament just four sets were played, as follows:

   Alan versus Bart   Alan versus Earl

   Clay versus Dick   Clay versus Earl

2. The winner of only one set was the same in both tournaments.
3. Alan won the first tournament.
4. In each tournament, only the winner of the tournament did not lose a set.

Who won the second tournament?

NOTE: *A tie is not possible in a set.*

Hint: Determine the winner of each set in the first tournament from the number of sets one man must have won; then determine which opponent lost against the same man in each tournament.

18

The Absent Digit

$$
\begin{array}{r}
A\ B\ C\ D \\
+ \quad\ \ B\ C\ D \\
\hline
E\ F\ G\ H\ I
\end{array}
$$

In the addition above, each letter represents a different digit.

Which one of the ten digits is absent?

HINT: Determine the possible values of B from the values of A, E, and F; then determine whether or not 1 was carried from $C + C$.

19

Interns' Week

Three interns are residents of the same hospital.

1. On only one day of the week are all three interns on call.
2. No intern is on call on three consecutive days.
3. No two interns are off on the same day more than once a week.
4. The first intern is off on Sunday, Tuesday, and Thursday.
5. The second intern is off on Thursday and Saturday.
6. The third intern is off on Sunday.

Which day of the week are all three interns on call?

Hint: Determine who is on call on Sunday, Tuesday, and Thursday; then determine who is off on each of three other days.

21

𝟚𝟘

The Lead

The sisters of Alex White were Bell and Cass; the brothers of his girl-friend, Faye Black, were Dean and Ezra. Their occupations were as follows:

	Alex: dancer		Dean: dancer
WHITE'S	Bell: dancer	BLACK'S	Ezra: singer
	Cass: singer		Faye: singer

One of the six was the lead in a movie; one of the other five was the director of the movie.

1. If the lead and the director were related, the director was a singer.
2. If the lead and the director were not related, the director was a man.
3. If the lead and the director had the same occupation, the director was a woman.
4. If the lead and the director had different occupations, the director was a White.
5. If the lead and the director were the same sex, the director was a dancer.
6. If the lead and the director were different sexes, the director was a Black.

Who was the lead?

HINT: From the premises and conclusions of the statements, determine which sets of three statements can be applicable.

22

21

The Drummer

Two women, Arlene and Cheryl, and two men, Burton and Donald, are musicians. One is a pianist, a second is a violinist, a third is a flutist, and a fourth is a drummer. On a day they were seated around a square table:

1. The person who sat across from Burton was the pianist.
2. The person who sat across from Donald was not the flutist.
3. The person who sat on Arlene's left was the violinist.
4. The person who sat on Cheryl's left was not the drummer.
5. The flutist and the drummer were married.

Who is the drummer?

HINT: Determine by names the different ways it is possible to seat the four people. Then determine which musical titles can be applied to the names without contradicting any statement.

Middle Apartment

Austin, Brooks, and Calvin lived on the same floor of an apartment building. One man's apartment was in the middle, adjacent to each of the other two men's apartments.

1. Each man owned only one pet: either a dog or a cat; each man drank only one beverage: either tea or coffee; and each man smoked only one form of tobacco: either a pipe or a cigar.
2. Austin lived next to a cigar-smoker.
3. Brooks lived next to a dog-owner.
4. Calvin lived next to a tea-drinker.
5. No pipe-smoker was a tea-drinker.
6. At least one cat-owner was a pipe-smoker.
7. At least one coffee-drinker lived next to a dog-owner.
8. No two designations such as cigar-smoker, dog-owner, tea-drinker, etc., belonged to more than one man.

Whose apartment was in the middle?

HINT: Determine the triplets of traits that can be associated with the three men; then determine the one triplet that can be associated with the man whose apartment is in the middle.

23

The Three Towns

Arlington, Burmingham, and Cantonville are three towns, each of which is shaped like a rectangle.

1. The number of blocks along the border of each town is a whole number; each block through each town is parallel to one pair of blocks along the border.
2. Arlington has the least number of blocks along its northern border, Burmingham has three more blocks along its northern border than Arlington has, and Cantonville has three more blocks along its northern border than Burmingham has.
3. The number of interior blocks through each of two of the towns equals the number of blocks along its entire border.

In which one of the three towns does the number of interior blocks through it not equal the number of blocks along its entire border?

NOTE: *A "block" refers to a length, not to an area.*

HINT: Find algebraic expressions for the number of blocks along an entire border and for the number of blocks through a town; equate the two expressions and look for whole-number solutions.

24

Face Orientation

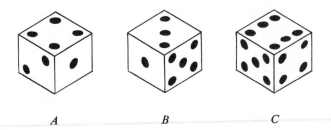

A	B	C

On a normal die, the sum of the numbers of spots on opposite faces is always seven; the three dice above are normal in that respect. However, two of the dice above are alike and one is different in respect to the orientation of the faces.

Which die—A, B, or C—is different?

NOTE: *If you find it difficult to visualize a die's six faces, you might draw a multiview die as shown below. The bottom face will be the only face not seen.*

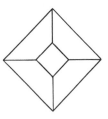

HINT: Orient the three cubes so that two similar adjoining faces occur in the same spatial positions; then determine the number of spots on the remaining faces.

𝟚𝟝

Change Required

Amos, Bert, Clem, and Dirk had just finished lunch in a restaurant and were paying their checks.

1. The four men, each of whose coins totaled one dollar, had the same number of silver coins.
2. Amos had exactly three quarters, Bert had exactly two quarters, Clem had exactly one quarter, and Dirk had no quarters.
3. The four men had to pay the same amount; three paid the exact amount, but the fourth required change.

Who required change?

NOTE: *"Silver coins" may be nickels, dimes, quarters, or half dollars.*

HINT: **Determine the number of coins held by each man; then determine what amounts cannot be paid exactly by all four men.**

26

The Doctor

Mr. Blank has a wife and a daughter; the daughter has a husband and a son. The following facts refer to the people mentioned:

1. One of the five people is a doctor and one of the other four is the doctor's patient.
2. The doctor's first offspring and the patient's older parent are of the same sex.
3. The doctor's first offspring is
   a. not the patient, and
   b. not the patient's older parent.

Who is the doctor?

27

Decapitation of a Product

$$
\begin{array}{r}
B\ C\ D\ E\ F\ A \\
\times \qquad\qquad M \\
\hline
A\ B\ C\ D\ E\ F
\end{array}
$$

In the multiplication above, each letter represents a different digit. Notice that if the "head" of the product falls to the rear it becomes the top factor.

Which one of the ten digits does M represent?

28

The Health Club

Ken and Liz met at a health club.

1a. Ken started going to the health club on the first Monday in January.
 b. Thereafter, Ken went every fifth day.
2a. Liz started going to the health club on the first Tuesday in January.
 b. Thereafter, Liz went every fourth day.
 3. Ken and Liz went to the health club on the same day just once in January; it was on that day that they met.

On which day of the month did Ken and Liz meet?

NOTE: *January has 31 days.*

HINT: Determine whether Liz started going before or after Ken started going; then determine on which dates Ken and Liz started going.

Dana's Death

Arlo, Bill, and Carl were questioned by a detective about the manner of Dana's death by drowning.

1. Arlo said: If it was murder, Bill did it.
2. Bill said: If it was murder, I did not do it.
3. Carl said: If it was not murder, it was suicide.
4. The detective said truthfully: If just one of these men lied, it was suicide.

What was the manner of Dana's death: accident, suicide, or murder ?

Hint: Determine the manner of Dana's death, assuming each of the statements [1] through [3] is false; then determine how many of these statements can be false altogether.

The Last to Row across Rapid River

Three men and two women crossed Rapid River in a boat that held only two persons.

1. No woman was left alone with a man at any time, as required by the women.
2. Only one person rowed during each crossing; no one rowed twice in succession, as required by the men.
3. Of those who rowed while alone in the boat, Art was the first, Ben was the second, and Cal was the third.

Who was the last to row across Rapid River?

NOTE: *Assume the minimum possible number of crossings.*

HINT: **Determine a way to cross the river so that only two men or two women are in the boat during a crossing from the initial side of the river.**

31

The Victim

Harry and his wife, Harriet, gave a dinner party to which they invited: his brother, Barry, and Barry's wife, Barbara; his sister, Samantha, and Samantha's husband, Samuel; and his neighbor, Nathan, and Nathan's wife, Natalie.

While they were all seated at the table, a bowl of soup was spilled on someone. The chairs were arranged around the table as in the diagram below.

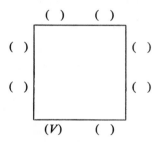

1. The victim of the spilled soup sat in the chair marked *V*.
2. Each man sat across from a woman.
3. Each man sat between a man and a woman.
4. No man sat across from his wife.
5. The host sat on the victim's right.
6. Barry sat next to the hostess.
7. Samantha sat next to the victim's spouse.

Who was the victim?

HINT: Determine a possible seating arrangement of men and women around the table without regard to specific people; then determine, beginning with the host's position, a possible seating arrangement of the particular men and women.

32

The Smallest Sum

I	II	III
G A L E	E L S A	N E A L
+ N E A L	+ G A L E	+ E L S A
E L S A	N E A L	G A L E

In each of the three additions above, each letter represents a different digit; however, each letter does not necessarily represent the same digit in one addition as it does in another addition.

Which addition—I, II, or III—has the smallest sum?

HINT: One letter in each addition behaves in a way peculiar to only one digit; determine this digit, then find two other digits associated with the one digit in each addition. To be specific, compare the first and third columns from the right in each addition.

33

Lee, Dale, Terry, and Marion

Lee, Dale, Terry, and Marion are related to each other, but not in-cestuously.

1. One is a different sex from the other three.
2. Among the four are Lee's mother, Dale's brother, Terry's father, and Marion's daughter.
3. The oldest and the youngest are of opposite sex.

Which one is a different sex from the other three?

34

The Punched-out Numeral

Two women and two men entered a cafeteria and each pulled a ticket, as illustrated below, from a machine.

50	95
45	90
40	85
35	80
30	75
25	70
20	65
15	60
10	55

1. The four ordered the same food and had the same numeral punched out on their tickets.
2. Each of the four had exactly four coins.
3. The two women had the same amount of money in coins, though no denomination of coin was held by both women; the two men had the same amount of money in coins, though no denomination of coin was held by both men.
4. Each of the four paid the exact amount indicated by the numeral that was punched out on his or her ticket.

Which numeral was punched out on each ticket ?

NOTE: "*Coins*" *may be pennies, nickels, dimes, quarters, half dollars, or silver dollars.*

HINT: **Determine a value for two sets of four coins where no coin denomination occurs in both sets; then determine another such value. Finally, determine the one amount that can be exactly paid from any of the four sets of four coins.**

35

The Professor

Amelia, Beulah, Carrie, Dennis, and Elwood attended a supper party with their spouses at Loverly's Restaurant. Chairs for the five couples were arranged around an L-shaped table as shown in the diagram below.

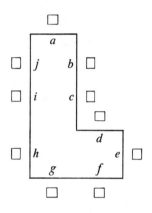

At the table:

1. Amelia's husband sat next to Dennis' wife.
2. Beulah's husband was the only man who sat alone at one side of the table.
3. Carrie's husband was the only man who sat between two women.
4. No woman sat between two women.
5. Each man sat opposite his wife.
6. Elwood's wife sat on the Professor's right.

Who was the Professor?

NOTE: *"Between two women" means to the left of one woman and to the right of another woman, around the perimeter of the table.*

HINT: Determine the seating arrangement of men and women around the table without necessarily regarding specific people; once this is done, the location of specific people becomes relatively easy.

37

36

Three J's

In the addition below, each letter represents a different digit.

$$
\begin{array}{r}
A\ B\ C \\
D\ E\ F \\
+\ G\ H\ I \\
\hline
J\ J\ J
\end{array}
$$

Which one of the ten digits does J represent?

NOTE: *Assume none of A, D, and G can be zero.*

HINT: Determine a possible sum for each column when J has a specific value; then test the sums by adding the three sums and J to see if the total is 45.

37

Escape from a Singleton

Doris, Laura, and Renee played two card games in which the objectives were: (a) to form pairs by drawing cards, and (b) to escape being left with a singleton.

The players took turns drawing a card from another player's hand; drawing continued until one player was left with the singleton. When a pair was formed after a drawing, the pair was discarded. After drawing a card from a second player's hand and discarding a pair, some player would be left with no cards at some point; in that event the third player would draw from the second player's hand when it was her turn to draw.

Near the end of each game:

1. Doris held just one card, Laura held just two cards, and Renee held just two cards; the combined hands contained two pairs and a singleton, but no one hand contained a pair.
2. Doris drew a card from Laura's hand and could not form a pair.
3. Laura was to draw a card from Renee's hand, after which Renee was to draw a card from Doris' hand.
4. No player was to hold the same hand twice in any one game.
5. The player who was to be left with the singleton was to be left with it for the first time.

Who escaped being left with the singleton in both games?

HINT: Determine the possible distributions of the cards in the three hands; then determine how a game could proceed so that no player held the same hand twice in any one game.

38

The Killer

The sisters of Aaron Green were Betty and Clara; the brothers of his girlfriend, Flora Brown, were Duane and Edwin. Their occupations were as follows:

	Aaron: doctor	Duane: doctor
GREEN'S	Betty: doctor	BROWN'S Edwin: lawyer
	Clara: lawyer	Flora: lawyer

One of the six killed one of the other five.

1. If the killer and the victim were related, the killer was a man.
2. If the killer and the victim were not related, the killer was a doctor.
3. If the killer and the victim had the same occupation, the victim was a man.
4. If the killer and the victim had different occupations, the victim was a woman.
5. If the killer and the victim were the same sex, the killer was a lawyer.
6. If the killer and the victim were different sexes, the victim was a doctor.

Who was the killer?

HINT: From the premises and conclusions of the statements, determine which sets of three statements can be applicable.

39

No Spade Played

A man and a woman played a card game in which (a) a player must play a card in the suit led, if possible, at each trick (otherwise, a player may play any card); and (b) a player who wins a trick must lead at the next trick.

1. The distribution of suits in the two hands was as follows:
     man's hand: spade–spade–heart–club
     woman's hand: diamond–diamond–heart–spade.
2. Each player led twice.
3. Each player won two tricks.
4. A different suit was led at each trick.
5. Two different suits were played at each trick.

At which trick—first, second, third, or fourth—was no spade played?

NOTE: *A trump had to win at least one trick. (A trump is any card in a certain suit that may be (a) played when a player has no cards in the suit led—in this event a card in the trump suit beats all cards in the other three suits; or (b) led, as any other suit may be led.)*

HINT: Determine the trump suit from a possible sequence of leads and wins; then determine at which trick the trump suit was led and won. Finally, determine the tricks at which a spade was played.

41

40

The Extortionist

Helen and her husband, Helmut, gave a dinner party to which they invited: her brother, Blair, and Blair's wife, Blanche; her sister, Sheila, and Sheila's husband, Sherman; and her neighbor, Nora, and Nora's husband, Norton. One of the eight was an extortionist and one of the other seven was the extortionist's victim.

While they were all seated at the table, the victim unsuccessfully attempted to stab the extortionist with a steak knife. The chairs were arranged around the table as in the diagram below.

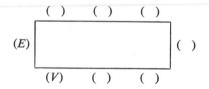

1. The extortionist sat in the chair marked *E*.
2. The victim sat in the chair marked *V*.
3. Each man sat across from a woman.
4. Each man sat between a man and a woman.
5. The extortionist's spouse and the victim's spouse sat next to each other.
6. The host sat between the victim and the hostess.
7. Blair sat between Sheila and Norton.

Who was the extortionist?

Hint: Determine the possible arrangements of men and women around the table without regard to specific people; then reduce these possible arrangements to only one, by gradually determining all the positions of the specific people.

The Unplaced Digits

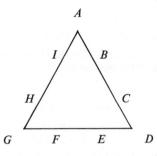

Moe placed nine of the ten digits, represented by letters in the diagram above, on each of two triangles.

1. The sum of the four digits along each side of a triangle was 14.
2. The digit not placed on the first triangle was different from the digit not placed on the second triangle.

Which two of the ten digits were not placed on both triangles?

Hint: Determine an equation that relates the sum of the corner digits, which are used twice in forming sums, to an unplaced digit. Then, from the possible corner digits, determine the possible corner digits. Finally, determine the intermediate digits.

Identified as the Criminal

At a police line-up a witness to a crime sought to identify a criminal from among four men. The witness looked for a man who was not tall, not fair, not skinny, and not good-looking; though looking for any of these characteristics may not have been valid.

In the line-up:
1. Four men each stood next to at least one tall man.
2. Exactly three men each stood next to at least one fair man.
3. Exactly two men each stood next to at least one skinny man.
4. Exactly one man stood next to at least one good-looking man.

Of the four men:
5. The first man was fair, the second man was skinny, the third man was tall, and the fourth man was good-looking.
6. No two men had more than one characteristic – tall, fair, skinny, good-looking – in common.
7. Just one man had more than two looked-for characteristics, i.e. not tall, not fair, not skinny, not good-looking; this man was identified as the criminal by the witness.

Which man—first, second, third, or fourth—was identified as the criminal by the witness?

HINT: Determine the possible positions of tall men, of fair men, of skinny men, and of a good-looking man in a four-man line-up. Then determine all possible characteristics of each man. Finally, choose the man with only one characteristic from among tall, fair, skinny, and good-looking.

43

The Last to Row across Limpid Lake

Four men and four women crossed Limpid Lake in a boat that held only three persons.

1. No woman was left alone with a man at any time, as required by the women.
2. Only one person rowed during each crossing; no one rowed twice in succession, as required by the men.
3. No woman rowed, as required by both the men and the women.
4. Of those who rowed, Abraham was the first, Barrett was the second, Clinton was the third, and Douglas was the fourth.
5. Only the person who rowed was in the boat during each return crossing to the original shore.

Who was the last to row across Limpid Lake?

NOTE: *Assume the minimum possible number of crossings.*

HINT: Determine a way to cross the lake so that a man, who did not row across the first time, will be able to row across the second time and so that a man, who did not row across the next-to-last time, will be able to row across the last time.

Card Number Six

Eight numbered cards lie face down on a table in the relative positions shown in the diagram below.

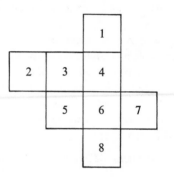

Of the eight cards:

1. Every Ace borders on a King.
2. Every King borders on a Queen.
3. Every Queen borders on a Jack.
4. No Queen borders on an Ace.
5. No two cards of the same kind border on each other.
6. There are two Aces, two Kings, two Queens, and two Jacks.

Which kind of card—Ace, King, Queen, or Jack—is card number six?

HINT: Assume card number six is either an Ace, a King, a Queen, or a Jack. In only one case does no contradiction arise concerning the number of each kind of card.

45

The Shortest Time

One evening Wilson, Xavier, Yeoman, Zenger, and Osborn made separate camps along the banks of a river. The next morning all were to meet at Osborn's camp; then each man besides Osborn was to return to his own camp.

1. Wilson and Xavier camped downstream from Osborn, while Yeoman and Zenger camped upstream from Osborn.
2. Wilson, Xavier, Yeoman, and Zenger each had a motor boat; each motor boat would take its owner to Osborn's camp in one hour, if there were no current in the river.
3. There was a strong current in the river.
4. The next morning each of the four men went in his motor boat to Osborn's camp; Wilson made the trip in 75 minutes, Xavier made the trip in 70 minutes, Yeoman made the trip in 50 minutes, and Zenger made the trip in 45 minutes.

Which one of the four men made the round trip, to and from Osborn's camp, in the shortest time?

HINT: Represent algebraically the time each man takes to go upstream and the time each man takes to go downstream; then determine the time it takes each man to return to his camp.

46

An Extraordinarily Empathic Man

Adam, Brad, and Cole are three extraordinary men, each having exactly three extraordinary characteristics.

1. Two are extraordinarily intelligent, two are extraordinarily handsome, two are extraordinarily strong, two are extraordinarily witty, and one is extraordinarily empathic.
2. Of Adam it is true that:
   a. if he is extraordinarily witty, he is extraordinarily handsome;
   b. if he is extraordinarily handsome, he is *not* extraordinarily intelligent.
3. Of Brad it is true that:
   a. if he is extraordinarily witty, he is extraordinarily intelligent;
   b. if he is extraordinarily intelligent, he is extraordinarily handsome.
4. Of Cole it is true that:
   a. if he is extraordinarily handsome, he is extraordinarily strong;
   b. if he is extraordinarily strong, he is *not* extraordinarily witty.

Who is extraordinarily empathic?

HINT: Determine the possible sets of characteristics for each man. Then assume either Adam, Brad, or Cole is empathic. In only one case does no contradiction arise concerning the possible sets of characteristics.

47

Old Maid

Dorothy, Loretta, and Rosalyn played a card game in which the objectives were (a) to form pairs by drawing cards, and (b) to escape being left with a singleton called the Old Maid.

The players took turns drawing a card from another player's hand; drawing continued until one player was left with the Old Maid. When a pair was formed after a drawing, the pair was discarded. After drawing a card from a second player's hand and discarding a pair, some player would be left with no cards at some point; in that event the third player would draw from the second player's hand when it was her turn to draw.

Near the end of the game:

1. Dorothy held just one card, Loretta held just two cards, and Rosalyn held just four cards; the combined hands contained three pairs and the Old Maid, but no hand contained a pair.
2. Dorothy drew from one of the other player's hands and could not form a pair.
3. The player, whose hand Dorothy had drawn from, was next to draw from the remaining player's hand.
4. No player was to hold the same hand twice.
5. The game was to last for just five drawings.

Who was left with the Old Maid?

HINT: Determine the distribution of the cards in the three hands; then determine how the game could proceed so that no player held the same hand twice and so that exactly five drawings occurred.

49

48

The Smiths

Two women, Audrey and Brenda, and two men, Conrad and Daniel, each do calisthenics on two days during a Sunday-through-Saturday period.

1. The second day on which Audrey does calisthenics is five days after the first day.
2. The second day on which Brenda does calisthenics is four days after the first day.
3. The second day on which Conrad does calisthenics is three days after the first day.
4. The second day on which Daniel does calisthenics is two days after the first day.
5a. The Smiths, consisting of one man and one woman, do calisthenics on the same day just once during a period.
5b. Of the remaining days, only one person does calisthenics on each day.

Who are the Smiths?

HINT: Determine four days the women could do calisthenics; then determine which man does calisthenics on each of three remaining days. Finally, determine a day when a woman does calisthenics that only one man can do calisthenics.

49

The Hired Man

Alden, Brent, Craig, and Derek applied for a job that required the applicant:

To be a high school graduate.

To have at least two years of previous work.

To be a veteran.

To have satisfactory references.

One man, who met more of the requirements than any of the other men, was hired.

1. Each of the six possible pairs of requirements was met by exactly one man.
2. Alden and Brent had the same amount of education.
3. Craig and Derek had the same amount of previous work.
4. Brent and Craig were both veterans.
5. Derek had satisfactory references.

Who was hired?

Then, if a requirement is met by a man, place an X in the appropriate box; and, if a requirement is not met by a man, place an O in the appropriate box. Eliminate those charts where the satisfying of a pair of requirements is not possible.

	A	B	C	D
g				
w				
a				
r				

HINT: Make charts like the one below where the capital letters represent the men and the other letters represent the requirements.

50

More Types of Crime

Mr. and Mrs. Astor, Mr. and Mrs. Brice, and Mr. and Mrs. Crane were seated around a table as shown below.

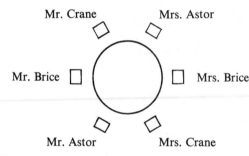

At the table:
1. Exactly three people sat next to at least one murderer.
2. Exactly four people sat next to at least one extortionist.
3. Exactly five people sat next to at least one swindler.
4. Six people sat next to at least one thief.

Of the types of crime:
5. No two people committed more than one type of crime in common.
6. One person committed more types of crime than each of the other persons.

Of the people:
7. Mr. and Mrs. Astor each committed exactly one type of crime, though not the same type.
8. Mr. and Mrs. Brice were both swindlers.
9. Mr. and Mrs. Crane were both thieves.
10. More women than men were swindlers.

Who committed more types of crime than each of the other persons?

Hint: Determine separately the possible seating arrangements of the murderers, of the extortionists, of the swindlers, and of the thieves. Then determine the number of persons who committed four types of crime, just three types of crime, just two types of crime, and just one type of crime. Finally determine the specific types of crime committed by each person.

SOLUTIONS

1 / Ham Yesterday, Pork Today

From [1] and [2], if Adrian orders ham, Buford orders pork and Carter orders pork. This situation contradicts [3]. So Adrian orders only pork.

Then, from [2], Carter orders only ham.

So only Buford could have ordered ham yesterday, pork today.

2 / Val, Lynn, and Chris

From [1], among the three are a father, a daughter, and a sibling. If Val's father were Chris, then Chris' sibling would have to be Lynn. Then, from [2], Lynn's daughter would have to be Val. So Val would be the daughter of both Lynn and Chris, and Lynn and Chris would be siblings. This relationship is incestuous and is not allowed.

So Val's father is Lynn. Then, from [2], Chris' sibling is Val. So Lynn's daughter is Chris. Then, from [1], Val is Lynn's son. *Therefore, Chris is the only female.*

3 / The Hospital Staff

From [1], [4], and the fact that there are 16 doctors and nurses, there are nine or more nurses and six or less male doctors. So, from [2], the division of the number of nurses according to sex must be such that the number of males is less than six.

From [3], the number of female nurses must be less than the number of male nurses. So there must be more than four male nurses.

Since there are less than six and more than four male nurses, there must be exactly five male nurses.

So there must be no more than nine nurses, consisting of five males and four females, and there must be no less than six male doctors. Then there must be only one female doctor to bring the total to 16.

If a male doctor is not included, [2] is contradicted. If a male nurse is not included, [3] is contradicted. If a female doctor is not included, [4] is contradicted. If a female nurse is not included, no fact is contradicted; *so the speaker is female and is a nurse.*

4 / The Woman Freeman Will Marry

From [1], [3], and [4], either Deb or Eve must be in the same age bracket as Ada and Cyd; so Ada and Cyd are under 30. From [7], Freeman will not marry Ada or Cyd.

From [2], [5], and [6], either Cyd or Deb must have the same occupation as Bea and Eve; so Bea and Eve are secretaries. From [7], Freeman will not marry Bea or Eve.

By elimination, *Freeman will marry Deb,* who must be over 30 and a teacher.

The remaining characteristics of the other four women can be determined from previous reasoning. Eve must be under 30 and Bea must be over 30. Cyd must be a secretary and Ada must be a teacher.

5 / Six A's

The sums $A + B + C$ and $A + D + E$ cannot be greater than 27 ($9 + 9 + 9$). G, H, and I represent different digits; so one number was carried from the right-hand column to the middle column, and a different number was carried from the middle column to the left-hand column. The only column sum, less than or equal to 27 for which this is true is 19. So the sums $A + B + C$ and $A + D + E$ must equal 19.

It follows that *FGHI* equals 2109.

What triplets of different digits result in a sum of 19, with no digit in the triplet equal to zero, 1, 2, or 9? Trial and error produces two such triplets: 4, 7, and 8; 5, 6, and 8. So *A represents 8.* The two possible additions are:

$$
\begin{array}{r}
8\,8\,8 \\
7\,7\,7 \\
+\,4\,4\,4 \\
\hline
2\,1\,0\,9
\end{array}
\qquad \text{and} \qquad
\begin{array}{r}
8\,8\,8 \\
6\,6\,6 \\
+\,5\,5\,5 \\
\hline
2\,1\,0\,9
\end{array}
$$

6 / Not Remarkably Rich

From [3] and [5], if Annette is intelligent she is artistic. From [5], if Annette is rich she is artistic. From [1] and [2], if Annette is neither rich nor intelligent she is artistic. So, in any case, Annette is artistic.

From [4], if Claudia is beautiful she is artistic. From [5], if Claudia is rich she is artistic. From [1] and [2], if Claudia is neither rich nor beautiful she is artistic. So, in any case, Claudia is artistic.

Then, from [1], Bernice is not artistic. Then, from [4], Bernice is not beautiful. So, from [1] and [2], Bernice is intelligent and rich.

Then, from [1], Annette and Claudia are both beautiful. Then, from [2] and [3], Annette is not intelligent; so, from [1], Claudia is intelligent. Then, from [1] and [2], Annette is rich and *Claudia is not rich.*

7 / The Tennis Player

From [3], there are four possible seating arrangements of the men and women (A represents Alice, B represents Brian, C represents Carol, and D represents David):

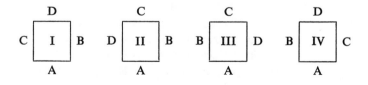

From [1] and [2], arrangements I and II are eliminated and III and IV become:

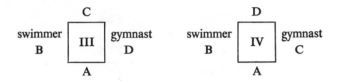

From [4], arrangement III is eliminated and the skater must be David. *So Alice is the tennis player.*

8 / The Round

From [1] and [2], at least five games were played; from [1] and [3], at most six games were played.

If just five games were played, the winner of the round would have won the first, third, and fifth games, from [2]. But from [3], [4], and [5], each man would have been the dealer for one of these games. This situation contradicts [6], so exactly six games were played.

Since exactly six games were played, Charles was the dealer for the last or sixth game, from [3], [4], and [5]. From [1], the winner of the last or sixth game won the round; so, from [6], Anthony or Bernard won the last or sixth game and, thus, the round.

If Anthony won the sixth game he could not have won the first game or the fourth game, from [6]; nor could he have won the fifth game, from [2]. Then he could only have won the second and third games, a situation which contradicts [2]. So Anthony did not win the sixth game.

Then Bernard must have won the sixth game and, thus, *Bernard won the round.*

There are four possible sequences of wins as shown below (A represents Anthony, B represents Bernard, and C represents Charles).

	dealer	A B C A B C
i	winner	B A B C A B
ii	winner	B C B C A B
iii	winner	B C A B A B
iv	winner	B C A B C B

9 / Three D's

$A \times CB = DDD$.

$A \times CB = D \times 111$.

$A \times CB = D \times 3 \times 37$.

So CB is 37 or 74 (2 × 37).

If CB is 37, $A = 3D$.

If CB is 74, $2A = 3D$.

So there are six possibilities for the values of A, B, C, and D; the possibilities are shown in the chart below.

	CB	D	A
(a)	37	1	3
(b)	37	2	6
(c)	37	3	9
(d)	74	2	3
(e)	74	4	6
(f)	74	6	9

Since each letter represents a different digit, possibilities (a), (c), and (e) are immediately eliminated.

Doing the actual multiplication in (b), (d), and (f) to determine E, F, and G in each case, one gets:

$$
\begin{array}{r} 6 \\ \times\ 37 \\ \hline 42 \\ 18 \\ \hline 222 \end{array}
\qquad
\begin{array}{r} 3 \\ \times\ 74 \\ \hline 12 \\ 21 \\ \hline 222 \end{array}
\qquad
\begin{array}{r} 9 \\ \times\ 74 \\ \hline 36 \\ 63 \\ \hline 666 \end{array}
$$

(b)   (d)   (f)

Only in (b) can each letter represent a different digit. *So D represents 2.*

10 / Lawyers' Testimony

At least one of statements [2] and [4] is true.

If both [2] and [4] are true, then Curtis killed Dwight and, from [I], statements [5] and [6] are both false. But if Curtis killed Dwight, [5] and [6] cannot both be false. So Curtis did not kill Dwight.

Then only one of statements [2] and [4] is true.

Then, from [II], it is impossible for just one of statements [1], [3], and [5] to be true, as required by [I]. So [1], [3], and [5] are all false and [6] is the other true statement.

Since [6] is true, a lawyer killed Dwight. Since

        Curtis did not kill Dwight from previous reasoning,

        Barney is not a lawyer because [3] is false, and

        Albert is a lawyer because [1] is false

it follows that

        [4] is true,

        [2] is false, and

        Albert killed Dwight.

11 / Spot Orientation

No matter which face a die rests on, the spots for one, four, and five have the same orientation. However, the spots for two, three, and six can have either of the following orientations:

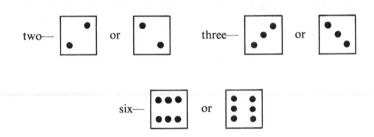

The following reasoning uses the fact that the sum of the numbers of spots on opposite faces is seven.

If die *B* were like die *A*, the two on die *B* would have an orientation opposite to that shown. So die *A* and die *B* are not alike.

If die *C* were like die *A*, the three on die *C* would have an orientation opposite to that shown. So die *A* and die *C* are not alike.

If die *C* were like die *B*, the six on die *C* would have an orientation the same as that shown.

Since it is stated that two dice are alike, die *B* and die *C* must be alike. *So die A is different.*

12 / Cora's Death

The following chart shows the manner of Cora's death according to whether the statements made by Anna and Beth are true or false.

	ANNA'S STATEMENT	BETH'S STATEMENT
True	murder by Beth or suicide or accident	murder or suicide
False	murder, but not by Beth	accident

Because the assumptions cover all possible situations with regard to the truth or falsity of the women's statements and because both assumptions cannot be applicable at the same time, only one assumption is applicable.

Assumption [1] cannot be applicable because Beth's statement cannot be true under its application. So assumption [2] is applicable.

Since assumption [2] is applicable, Beth's statement cannot be false; so only Anna's statement is false. *Then the manner of Cora's death must have been murder.*

13 / A Chair for Mr. Lancer

From [3] and [4], the arrangement around the table could have been only one of the following (M represents man and W represents woman):

```
        M                        M
      W   W                    W   W
    W       W    or          W       W
    W       M                M       W
      M   M                    M   M
        M                        M
```

From [2], a woman sat in chair *a*. Then, from [1] and [2], the partial seating arrangement was either:

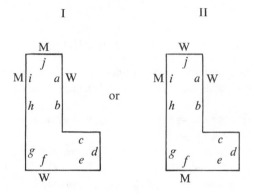

From the arrangement deduced from [3] and [4], men must have sat in chairs *g* and *h* in I. Also, a woman could not have sat in chair *h* in II: a man would have sat in chair *b*, from [1], and a woman would have sat in chair *g*, from [3]; this situation contradicts the arrangement deduced from [3] and [4]. Thus, men must have sat in chairs *h* and *g* in II. So, from the above reasoning and from [1], the partial seating arrangement becomes either:

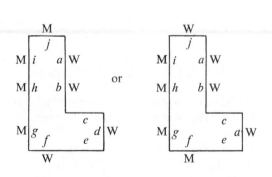

Then, from the fact that only one woman sat between two women (see first diagram) and from [1], the complete arrangement was either:

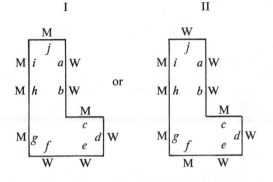

So, in any case, **Mr. Lancer sat in chair c,** from [4].

14 / Decapitation of a Factor

M is greater than 1 and $M \times A$ is less than 10; so, if A is not 1, M and A have one of the following pairs of values: (a) 2 and 4, or (b) 2 and 3.

Substituting for M and A, one seeks values for F such that $M \times F$ ends in A. Upon finding a suitable value for F, one then seeks a value for E such that $M \times E$, plus whatever is carried, ends in F. And so on. One finds in (a) that when M is 2 no value exists for D, and when M is 4 no value exists for D or E; in (b) that when M is 2 no value exists for F, but when M is 3 a suitable multiplication occurs. The multiplication is shown below.

$$\begin{array}{r} 2\,8\,5\,7\,1\,4 \\ \times \quad\quad\quad 3 \\ \hline 8\,5\,7\,1\,4\,2 \end{array}$$

The reasoning above assumed A was not 1. If A is 1, then either M or F is 7 and the other is 3. When M is 7, both E and F are 3; but when M is 3 a suitable multiplication occurs. The multiplication is shown below.

$$\begin{array}{r} 1\,4\,2\,8\,5\,7 \\ \times \quad\quad\quad 3 \\ \hline 4\,2\,8\,5\,7\,1 \end{array}$$

So, in any case, **M is 3.**

15 / The Singleton

From [2], there were four pairs in the combined hands. Then, from [3], Lois' and Dora's hands formed three pairs, Lois' and Rose's hands formed one pair, and Rose's and Dora's hands formed no pairs.

So, from the above reasoning, the pairs were distributed as follows (*A*, *B*, *C*, and *D* represent one of a pair):

LOIS' HAND	DORA'S HAND	ROSE'S HAND
ABCD	*ABC*	*D*

From [1] and the fact that there were 35 cards, Lois and Rose each were dealt 12 cards and Dora was dealt 11 cards. So, after the pairs were removed, Dora held an odd number of cards while Lois and Rose each held an even number of cards. *Thus, the singleton must have been in Rose's hand.*

16 / The Sisters

Using [1] and [2], one discovers by trial and error that the four holdings were as follows (H represents half dollar, Q represents quarter, D represents dime, and N represents nickel):

60¢		75¢	
I	Q Q D	III	H N N N N N
II	N N H	IV	Q D D D D D

Then, from [3] and [4], Cindy's holding must be IV. Then, from [3] and [4], Betsy's holding must be III. Then, from [3] and [4], Delia's holding must be II. Then, from [3] and [4], Agnes' holding must be I.

So, after paying their checks, the women had coins as follows:

Agnes (I)—Q Q	Betsy (III)—H N
Delia (II)—N	Cindy (IV)—D D D

So, from [5], *the two sisters were Agnes and Betsy.*

17 / The Second Tournament

From [1], Alan, Clay, and Earl each played two sets; so, from [4], each won at least one set in each tournament. From [3] and [4], Alan won two sets in the first tournament; then Clay and Earl each won one set in the first tournament. The winners of the sets in the first tournament, then, are as follows (the winner is represented by a name in capital letters)

ALAN versus Bart	ALAN versus Earl (4th set)
CLAY versus Dick	Clay versus EARL (3rd set)

From [2] and the fact that Alan won at least one set in the second tournament, Alan must have either won against Earl again or won against Bart again. If Alan won against Earl again, Earl would have to have won against Clay again, which contradicts [2]. So Alan did not win against Earl again but did win against Bart again. Then the winners of the sets in the second tournament are as follows:

ALAN versus Bart (1st set)	Alan versus EARL (2nd set)
Clay versus DICK (4th set)	CLAY versus Earl (3rd set)

In the second tournament, only Dick did not lose a set; so, from [4], **Dick won the second tournament.**

NOTE: *The sets may be ordered as shown, if the loss of a set is considered as eliminating a player from further competition.*

18 / The Absent Digit

Because at least 1 must have been carried from $B + B$ and because at most 1 can be carried, A is 9, E is 1, and F is zero.

Then B is greater than 4.

If B is 5 then G is zero or G is 1, contradicting the fact that each letter represents a different digit. So B is not 5.

Then B is 6, 7, or 8. If B is 6, G is 2 or 3. If B is 7, G is 4 or 5. If B is 8, G is 6 or 7. The possibilities so far, then, are as follows.

	(i)	(ii)	(iii)
	9 6 C D	9 6 C D	9 7 C D
	+ 6 C D	+ 6 C D	+ 7 C D
	1 0 2 $H I$	1 0 3 $H I$	1 0 4 $H I$

	(iv)	(v)	(vi)
	9 7 C D	9 8 C D	9 8 C D
	+ 7 C D	+ 8 C D	+ 8 C D
	1 0 5 $H I$	1 0 6 $H I$	1 0 7 $H I$

In (i), (iii), and (v), nothing was carried from $C + C$; so C must be less than 5. In (ii), (iv), and (vi), 1 was carried from $C + C$; so C must be greater than 4. Using this information, one finds the above possibilities expand to fifteen in number.

(i a)	(i b)	(ii a)	(ii b)	(ii c)
9 6 3 D	9 6 4 D	9 6 7 D	9 6 7 D	9 6 8 D
+ 6 3 D	+ 6 4 D	+ 6 7 D	+ 6 7 D	+ 6 8 D
1 0 2 7 I	1 0 2 8 I	1 0 3 4 I	1 0 3 5 I	1 0 3 7 I

(iii a)	(iii b)	(iv a)	(iv b)	(iv c)
9 7 2 D	9 7 3 D	9 7 6 D	9 7 6 D	9 7 8 D
+ 7 2 D	+ 7 3 D	+ 7 6 D	+ 7 6 D	+ 7 8 D
1 0 4 5 I	1 0 4 6 I	1 0 5 2 I	1 0 5 3 I	1 0 5 6 I

(v a)	(v b)	(v c)	(vi a)	(vi b)
9 8 2 D	9 8 2 D	9 8 3 D	9 8 6 D	9 8 6 D
+ 8 2 D	+ 8 2 D	+ 8 3 D	+ 8 6 D	+ 8 6 D
1 0 6 4 I	1 0 6 5 I	1 0 6 7 I	1 0 7 2 I	1 0 7 3 I

Continuing to use the previous reasoning, one finds that eleven possibilities are eliminated and only four additions are possible.

(iii a)	(iv a)	(iv c)	(v b)
9 7 2 8	9 7 6 4	9 7 8 2	9 8 2 7
+ 7 2 8	+ 7 6 4	+ 7 8 2	+ 8 2 7
1 0 4 5 6	1 0 5 2 8	1 0 5 6 4	1 0 6 5 4

So, in any case, *3 is the absent digit.*

19 / Interns' Week

From [4] and [5], the first and second interns are off on Thursday and, from [4] and [6], the first and third interns are off on Sunday. So, from [3], the second intern is on call on Sunday and the third intern is on call on Thursday.

From [4], the first intern is off on Tuesday. So, from [3], the second and third interns are on call on Tuesday.

This information can be put into chart form as shown below (X represents on call and – represents off):

	SUN	MON	TUES	WED	THURS	FRI	SAT
1st intern	–		–		–		
2nd intern	X		X		–		
3rd intern	–		X		X		

From [2], the second intern is off on Monday and the third intern is off on Wednesday. From [5], the second intern is off on Saturday. So, from [1], *Friday is the day all three interns are on call.*

The chart may be completed as follows. From [2], the third intern is off on Saturday. From [3], the first intern is on call on Monday, Wednesday, and Saturday; the second intern is on call on Wednesday; and the third intern is on call on Monday.

20 / The Lead

From their premises, just one of [1] and [2], just one of [3] and [4], and just one of [5] and [6] are applicable. From their conclusions, [1] and [5] cannot both be applicable, [2] and [3] cannot both be applicable, and [4] and [6] cannot both be applicable. So either [1], [3], and [6] are applicable or [2], [4], and [5] are applicable.

If [1], [3], and [6] are applicable, then from their conclusions the director was Faye, a Black woman singer. Then from their premises the lead was Ezra, a Black man singer.

If [2], [4], and [5] are applicable, then from their conclusions the director was Alex, a White man dancer. Then from their premises the lead was Ezra, a Black man singer.

So, in any case, *Ezra was the lead.*

21 / The Drummer

There are six possible seating arrangements of the men and women (A represents Arlene, B represents Burton, C represents Cheryl, and D represents Donald):

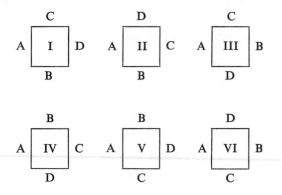

From [1] and [3], arrangements I and II are eliminated and III, IV, V, and VI become:

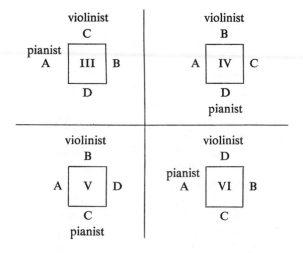

From [5], arrangements III and IV are eliminated. From [2], arrangements V and VI become:

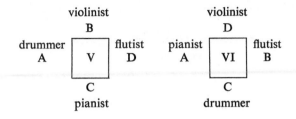

From [4], arrangement V is eliminated and ***the drummer must be Cheryl.***

22 / Middle Apartment

From [1], one of the following sets of triplets is associated with each man:

(i) coffee, dog, cigar   (v) coffee, dog, pipe

(ii) coffee, cat, pipe   (vi) coffee, cat, cigar

(iii) tea, dog, pipe   (vii) tea, dog, cigar

(iv) tea, cat, cigar   (viii) tea, cat, pipe

From [5], triplets (iii) and (viii) are eliminated. Then, from [6], triplet (ii) is one of the triplets. Then, from [8], triplets (v) and (vi) are eliminated. Then, from [8], triplets (iv) and (vii) cannot both be possible; so triplet (i) is one of the triplets. Then, from [8], triplet (vii) is eliminated; so triplet (iv) is the remaining triplet.

From [2], [3], and [4], the man whose apartment is in the middle either:

    I. is a cigar-smoker and a dog-owner,

   II. is a cigar-smoker and a tea-drinker, or

   III. is a dog-owner and a tea-drinker.

Since the triplets are (i), (ii), and (iv), the "middle" triplet must be either (i) or (iv) as shown below.

(ii)	(i)	(iv)		(ii)	(iv)	(i)
coffee	coffee	tea		coffee	tea	coffee
cat	dog	cat	or	cat	cat	dog
pipe	cigar	cigar		pipe	cigar	cigar

From [7], triplet (iv) cannot be the "middle" one; so, from [4], *Calvin's apartment was in the middle.*

23 / The Three Towns

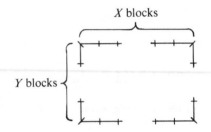

Let X equal the number of blocks along each of two opposite sides of the two towns mentioned in [3], and let Y equal the number of blocks along each of the other two opposite sides. Then the number of blocks along an entire border is equal to $X + Y + X + Y$ or $2X + 2Y$, and the number of blocks through a town is equal to X times $(Y - 1)$ plus Y times $(X - 1)$ or $(XY - X) + (XY - Y)$.

From [3], let $2X + 2Y = XY - X + XY - Y$ for the two towns. Solving for X, $X = 3Y/(2Y - 3)$. Solving for Y, $Y = 3X/(2X - 3)$. Thus, X and Y must both be greater than 1. Letting Y be 2, 3, 4, 5, 6, and 7 in turn, one gets the following values:

Y	X
2	6
3	3
4	$\frac{12}{5}$
5	$\frac{15}{7}$
6	2
7	$\frac{21}{11}$

Since X must be greater than 1 and, from [1], a whole number, there are no other values for X that are whole numbers.

From [1] and the above values, the number of blocks along one side of each of the two towns is either 2, 3, or 6. From [2], Arlington has 3 blocks along its northern border, Burmingham has 6 blocks along its northern border, and Cantonville has 9 blocks along its northern border.

Since it is not possible for a town with 9 blocks along its northern border to satisfy the equation expressing condition [3], **Cantonville is the town that has the number of blocks through it not equal to the number of blocks along its border.**

In summary, Arlington has 12 blocks along its border and 12 blocks through it, and Burmingham has 16 blocks along its border and 16 blocks through it.

24 / Face Orientation

Using a multiview drawing of each die, one can write the number of spots on each face shown, as follows:

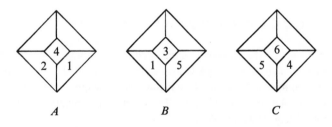

Then, using the fact that the sum of the numbers of spots on opposite faces is seven, one gets:

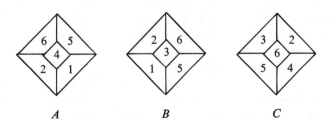

The numbers 2, 5, and 6 occur in each drawing and, by rotating the dice, can be shown on corresponding faces to get:

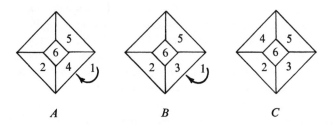

It now becomes evident that die *A* has its faces oriented differently from die *B* and from die *C*. *So die A is different.*

25 / Change Required

From [2], Amos had three quarters. So, from [1], Amos had either (*Q* represents quarter, *D* represents dime, and *N* represents nickel):

$$Q\,Q\,Q\,D\,D\,N, \quad Q\,Q\,Q\,D\,N\,N\,N, \text{ or } Q\,Q\,Q\,N\,N\,N\,N.$$

Then, from [1], the number of coins each man had was either six, seven, or eight. Trial and error reveals that a combination of six coins with two quarters and a combination of eight coins with one quarter are impossible. So the number of coins is seven. The different combinations are shown below (*H* represents half dollar).

SIX COINS	SEVEN COINS	EIGHT COINS
$Q\,Q\,Q\,D\,D\,N$	$Q\,Q\,Q\,D\,N\,N\,N$	$Q\,Q\,Q\,N\,N\,N\,N$
$Q\,Q\,?\,?\,?\,?$	$Q\,Q\,D\,D\,D\,D\,D$	$Q\,Q\,D\,D\,D\,D\,N\,N$
$Q\,H\,D\,N\,N$	$Q\,H\,N\,N\,N\,N$	$Q\,?\,?\,?\,?\,?\,?\,?$
$H\,D\,D\,D\,D\,D$	$H\,D\,D\,D\,D\,N\,N$	$H\,D\,D\,D\,N\,N\,N\,N$

Then, from [3], the amount in cents of each check was one of the following: 5, 10, 15, 20, 25, 30, 35, 40, 45, 50, 55, 60, 65, 70, 75, 80, 85, 90, 95, 100. Assuming the amount of each check was each amount in turn, one discovers that all four men could have paid the exact amount in all cases except when the amount in cents was 5, 15, 85, or 95. If the amount in cents was 5, 15, 85, or 95, only the man with two quarters, Bert, could not have paid exactly. *So Bert required change.*

26 / The Doctor

From [2], the doctor has a first offspring among the five people; so the doctor can be anybody but the daughter's son. Also from [2], the patient has a parent among the five people; so the patient is either the daughter or the daughter's son.

From [3a], if Mr. Blank or his wife is the doctor, his daughter is not the patient; while if his daughter or his daughter's husband is the doctor, his daughter's son is not the patient.

So one of the following must be the doctor-patient pair:

DOCTOR	PATIENT
A. Mr. Blank	his daughter's son
B. his wife	his daughter's son
C. his daughter	his daughter
D. his daughter's husband	his daughter

Pair C is eliminated from [1].

For pair A and pair B, the doctor's first offspring is Mr. Blank's daughter; but, from [2], the patient's older parent is also Mr. Blank's daughter. This situation contradicts [3b]; so pair A and pair B are eliminated.

Pair D must be the correct pair and *the doctor is the husband of Mr. Blank's daughter.* This conclusion is supported by the fact that the doctor's first offspring and the patient's older parent can be different males, as required by [2] and [3b].

27 / Decapitation of a Product

From the stipulation: M is not zero or 1, and $M \times B$ is less than 10; A is greater than M, M cannot be 9, and A must be greater than 2. So the set of values for M, A, B, and F must be one of the following:

	a	b	c	d		e	f		g		h		i		j
M	8	7	7	6	6	6	6	5	5	5	5	4	4	4	4	4
A	9	8	9	7	8	9	6	7	8	9	5	6	7	8	9
B	1	1	1	1	1	1	1	1	1	1	1	1	1	2	2
F	2	6	3	2	8	4	0	5	0	5	0	4	8	2	6

	k	l	m	n		o			p	q	r
M	3	3	3	3	3	3	2	2	2	2	2	2	2
A	4	5	6	7	8	9	3	4	5	6	7	8	9
B	1	1	2	2	2	3	1	2	2	3	3	4	4
F	2	5	8	1	4	7	6	8	0	2	4	6	8

The unlettered cases are eliminated because of duplicate values.

To find out which set of values gives unique values for the remaining letters, one proceeds as follows. One multiplied $M \times A$ to get F. Similarly, one multiplies $M \times F$, adding whatever was carried, to get E. And so on. If one gets a value for a letter that is not unique, one eliminates that set.

It turns out that only set j is not eliminated; one gets:

$$
\begin{array}{r}
230769 \\
\times \quad 4 \\
\hline
923076
\end{array}
$$

So M is 4.

28 / The Health Club

From [1a] and [2a], Liz started going to the health club either:

A. The day after Ken started going.

B. Six days before Ken started going.

If A is true, then from [1b] and [2b], Ken and Liz went to the health club on the same day at their second visits and again 20 days later. The second day they were at the health club together must have been in February, from [3]. But the latest days Ken and Liz could have started going are the 6th and 7th respectively; even at these latest days, they must have gone twice to the health club on the same day: on January 11th and on January 31st. So A is false and B is true.

For B, the first Tuesday cannot be later than the 1st; otherwise, the

Monday that follows will be the second Monday of the month. So Liz started going on the 1st and Ken started going on the 7th. Then, from [1b] and [2b], the days of the month each went were:

Liz: 1st, 5th, 9th, 13th, 17th, 21st, 25th, and 29th
Ken: 7th, 12th, 17th, 22nd, and 27th.

So, from [3], *Ken and Liz met on the 17th.*

29 / Dana's Death

The following chart shows the manner of Dana's death assuming each of statements [1] through [3] is false.

If False	STATEMENT [1]	STATEMENT [2]	STATEMENT [3]
	murder, but not by Bill	murder by Bill	accident

The chart reveals that no two statements can be false. So either none or one is false.

From [4], just one man could not have lied. So no man lied.

Since no man lied, it was neither murder nor an accident. *So the manner of Dana's death was suicide.*

NOTE: *It may seem strange that [1] and [2] are true together; that it was suicide, even though [4] is true. The reason this situation exists is as follows: when a premise in a statement is false, the statement as a whole is true— regardless of the truth or falsity of the conclusion.*

30 / The Last to Row across Rapid River

From [1] and [3], the crossings were accomplished in one of the following ways (W represents woman, M represents man, a represents Art, b represents Ben, and c represents Cal):

I			II		
(i) M_cWW	$M_aM_b \rightarrow$		(i) $M_?WW$	$M_aM_? \rightarrow$	
(ii) $M_cWW \leftarrow M_a$		M_b	(ii) $M_?WW \leftarrow M_a$		$M_?$
(iii) M_aM_c	WW	$\rightarrow M_b$	(iii) WW	$M_aM_? \rightarrow M_?$	
(iv) $M_aM_c \leftarrow M_b$		WW	(iv) WW	$\leftarrow M_b$	M_aM_c

(v) $M_?$	$M_?M_c \rightarrow WW$	(v) M_b	$WW \rightarrow M_aM_c$
(vi) $M_?$	$\leftarrow M_c$ $M_?WW$	(vi) M_b	$\leftarrow M_c$ M_aWW
(vii)	$M_?M_c \rightarrow M_?WW$	(vii)	$M_bM_c \rightarrow M_aWW$

From [2], neither Ben nor Cal could have rowed during crossing (v) in I; so Art did. Then, from [2], Ben rowed last in I. From [2], Ben rowed last in II. So, in any case, **Ben rowed last.**

To complete the details in I and II: from [2], neither Art nor Ben could have rowed during crossing (iii) in II, so Cal did. Then, from [2], Ben rowed first in II. From [2], Ben rowed first in I.

31 / The Victim

Trial and error, using [2] and [3], reveals that the men and women sat around the table in one of the following arrangements (M represents man and W represents woman):

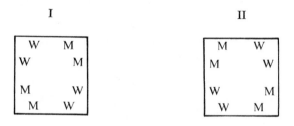

I

W	M
W	M
M	W
M	W

II

M	W
M	W
W	M
W	M

From [1] and [5], arrangement II is the correct one.

Then, from [4] and [6], Barry and the hostess must be seated in one of the following ways:

IIa

M	W	
M	W	hostess
W	M	Barry
W	M	

victim   host

IIb

	M	W
Barry	M	W
hostess	W	M
	W	M

victim   host

Then, from [4] and [7], Samantha and the victim's spouse must be seated in one of the following ways (curved lines indicate the married couples):

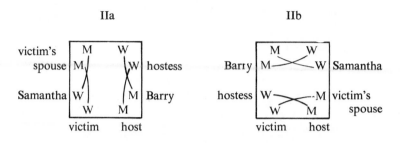

In each arrangement, *only Natalie can be the victim.* The two complete possible seating arrangements are shown below.

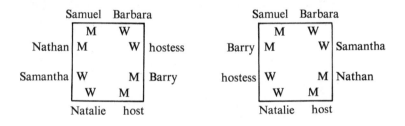

32 / The Smallest Sum

The E in addition I, the A in addition II, and the L in addition III all behave in the same way.

In I, either:	In II, either:	In III, either:
$\begin{cases} E + L = A \\ E + A = 10 + L \end{cases}$	$\begin{cases} A + E = L \\ A + L = 10 + E \end{cases}$	$\begin{cases} L + A = E \\ L + E = 10 + A \end{cases}$
or	or	or
$\begin{cases} E + A = L \\ E + L = 10 + A \end{cases}$	$\begin{cases} A + L = E \\ A + E = 10 + L \end{cases}$	$\begin{cases} L + E = A \\ L + A = 10 + E \end{cases}$

Only the digit 5 behaves in this way. For example:

$$5 + 3 = 8 \qquad 5 + 4 = 9$$
$$5 + 8 = 10 + 3 \qquad 5 + 9 = 10 + 4$$

So one gets:

I	II	III
$G\,A\,L\,5$	$E\,L\,S\,5$	$N\,E\,A\,5$
$+\,N\,5\,A\,L$	$+\,G\,5\,L\,E$	$+\,E\,5\,S\,A$
$5\,L\,S\,A$	$N\,E\,5\,L$	$G\,A\,5\,E$

A substitution for L in I, for E in II, and for A in III yields a value for A in I, for L in II, and for E in III. Trial and error produces (in the eliminated cases, 1 is carried from the second column to the third column, making the substitution invalid):

I (a) $G\,6\,1\,5$ (b) $G\,7\,2\,5$ (c) $G\,1\,6\,5$
   $+\,N\,5\,6\,1$ $+\,N\,5\,7\,2$ $+\,N\,5\,1\,6$
   $5\,1\,7\,6$ $5\,2\,9\,7$ $5\,6\,8\,1$

II (a) $6\,1\,S\,5$ (b) $7\,2\,S\,5$ (c) $8\,3\,S\,5$ (d) $9\,4\,S\,5$
   $+\,G\,5\,1\,6$ $+\,G\,5\,2\,7$ $+\,G\,5\,3\,8$ $+\,G\,5\,4\,9$
   $N\,6\,5\,1$ $N\,7\,5\,2$ $N\,8\,5\,3$ $N\,9\,5\,4$

III (a) $N\,6\,1\,5$ (b) $N\,7\,2\,5$ (c) $N\,8\,3\,5$ (d) $N\,9\,4\,5$
   $+\,6\,5\,S\,1$ $+\,7\,5\,S\,2$ $+\,8\,5\,S\,3$ $+\,9\,5\,S\,4$
   $G\,1\,5\,6$ $G\,2\,5\,7$ $G\,3\,5\,8$ $G\,4\,5\,9$

Inspection of the partial additions reveals that *I has the smallest sum.*

The additions can be completed further. The values of the remaining letters must be different from the values already present in each addition, Also, no first letter can be zero. So there are four possible additions for I, only one possible addition for II, and two possible additions for III, as shown below.

I (b) 1 7 2 5   (b) 3 7 2 5   (c) 2 1 6 5   (c) 3 1 6 5
       +3 5 7 2   +1 5 7 2   +3 5 1 6   +2 5 1 6
       ‾‾‾‾‾‾‾   ‾‾‾‾‾‾‾   ‾‾‾‾‾‾‾   ‾‾‾‾‾‾‾
        5 2 9 7   5 2 9 7   5 6 8 1   5 6 8 1

II (a) 6 1 3 5
        +2 5 1 6
        ‾‾‾‾‾‾‾
         8 6 5 1

III (a) 2 6 1 5   (b) 1 7 2 5
         +6 5 4 1   +7 5 3 2
         ‾‾‾‾‾‾‾   ‾‾‾‾‾‾‾
          9 1 5 6   9 2 5 7

33 / Lee, Dale, Terry, and Marion

The reasoning that follows uses the information in [2]. Lee's mother and Marion's daughter are either the same person or different persons.

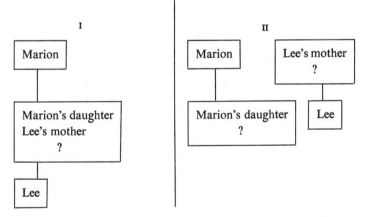

If the same person, then the partial situation can be represented as follows:

If different persons, then the partial situation can be represented as follows:

In I, Dale's brother is either Lee or Marion. So Terry is Lee's mother and Marion's daughter, and Terry's father is either Marion or Dale. Terry's father cannot be Dale because Dale's brother is either Lee or Marion. So Terry's father is Marion. Now suppose Dale's brother is Lee. Then, from

[1], Dale is a man, which contradicts [3]. So Dale's brother is Marion. From [3], Dale and Lee are both women. So Marion is the only male in I.

In II, Dale's brother and Terry's father must be the same person and the only male, from [1]. So Marion must be Terry's father and Dale's brother, which means Marion is the only male in II.

So, in any case, **Marion is the only male.**

34 / The Punched-out Numeral

Using [2] and [3], one finds by trial and error that only pairs of sets for 40 cents, 80 cents, 125 cents, and 130 cents are possible; the sets are as follows (S represents silver dollar, H represents half dollar, Q represents quarter, D represents dime, and N represents nickel):

D D D D	D D D H	Q Q Q H	D D D S
Q N N N	Q N Q Q	N D D S	Q N H H

One finds, by using [1] and [4], that only 30¢ and 100¢ can be paid exactly from 2 pairs of sets. But there is no 100 on a ticket. So, **the numeral punched out must have been 30.**

35 / The Professor

From [2], only one of chairs a, d, and e was occupied by a man. So, from [2] and [5], the partial seating arrangement was one of the following (M represents man and W represents woman):

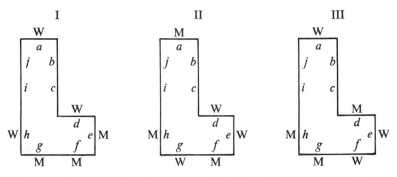

In I, Carrie's husband sat in chair b, c, i, or j, from [3]. However, from

[5], it is impossible for Carrie's husband to be the *only* man who sat between two women. So arrangement I is eliminated.

In II, a man already sits between two women in chair *f*. So, from [3], he must be Carrie's husband. Then a man would have to sit in chair *i*, in order that Carrie's husband be the only man to sit between two women. But then a woman would have to sit in chair *c*, from [5], leading to a contradiction of [4]. So arrangement II is eliminated.

So III is the correct arrangement.

In III, a man must have sat in chair *c*, from [2] and [3]; so a woman sat in chair *i*, from [5]. A woman cannot have sat in chair *j*, from [4]; so a man sat in chair *j* and this man is Carrie's husband, from [3]. Finally, a woman sat in chair *b*, from [5]. Then the partial seating arrangement becomes:

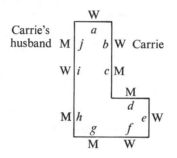

Then, from [2], Beulah's husband sat in chair *d*. Then, from [1] and [5], Amelia's husband sat in chair *h* and Dennis' wife sat in chair *i*. Then, from [5], Elwood's wife sat in chair *a*. Then, from [6], **the Professor was Carrie**.

In summary, the complete seating arrangement was the following:

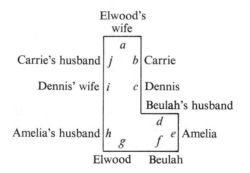

36 / Three J's

(i) Since A, D, and G represent three different digits, none of which can be zero, J must be 6, 7, 8, or 9.

(ii) Since C, F, and I represent three different digits, their sum cannot exceed 24; then, in order that J be 6, 7, 8, or 9, their sum cannot exceed 19.

(iii) If any two columns sum to 6, 7, 8, or 9, the third column must sum to 6, 7, 8, or 9; but, since A through I represent nine different digits, this situation is impossible. So at most one column sums to 6, 7, 8, or 9.

The following conclusions result from (i), (ii), and (iii).

(a) If $A + D + G$ sums to 6, then $C + F + I$ must sum to 16, 7, or 17.

(b) If $A + D + G$ sums to 7, then $C + F + I$ must sum to 17, 8, or 18.

(c) If $A + D + G$ sums to 8, then $C + F + I$ must sum to 18, 9, or 19.

(d) If $A + D + G$ sums to 9, then $C + F + I$ must sum to 19.

The sum for $B + E + H$ can be deduced from (a), (b), (c), and (d) to yield the following chart:

	$A + D + G$	$B + E + H$	$C + F + I$	J
I	6	5	16	6
II	6	17	7	7
III	6	16	17	7
IV	7	6	17	7
V	7	18	8	8
VI	7	17	18	8
VII	8	7	18	8
VIII	8	19	9	9
IX	8	18	19	9
X	9	8	19	9

Only for cases VIII and X does the sum of the terms in the four columns total 45 as they should. *So J must represent 9.*

Further investigation reveals the following possible combinations.

	$A + D + G$	$B + E + H$	$C + F + I$
VIII	$1 + 3 + 4$	$5 + 6 + 8$	$0 + 2 + 7$
	$1 + 2 + 5$	$4 + 7 + 8$	$0 + 3 + 6$
X	$2 + 3 + 4$	$0 + 1 + 7$	$5 + 6 + 8$
	$1 + 3 + 5$	$0 + 2 + 6$	$4 + 7 + 8$
	$1 + 2 + 6$	$0 + 3 + 5$	$4 + 7 + 8$

37 / Escape from a Singleton

From [1], one of the following situations must exist (A and B represent one of a pair, while S represents the singleton):

	DORIS' HAND	LAURA'S HAND	RENEE'S HAND
I	A	AB	BS
II	A	BS	AB
III	S	AB	AB

Then, from [2], [3], and [4], the drawings proceeded in any of the following orders:

I			IIa			IIb		
A	AB	BS	A	BS	AB	A	BS	AB
AB	A	BS	AB	S	AB	AS	B	AB
AB	AS	B	AB	AS	B	AS	AB	B
B	AS	AB						

IIc			III		
A	BS	AB	S	AB	AB
AS	B	AB	SA	B	AB
AS	$\cancel{BB}$	A	SA	$\cancel{BB}$	A
S	—	$\cancel{AA}$	A	—	SA
			$\cancel{AA}$	—	S

Orders I, IIa, and IIb cannot be completed, from [4]; so these orders are eliminated.

From [5], order IIc must have occurred in one game and order III must have occurred in the other game. Then Doris and Renee were both left with the singleton. *So Laura escaped being left with the singleton.*

38 / The Killer

From their premises, just one of [1] and [2], just one of [3] and [4], and just one of [5] and [6] are applicable. From their conclusions, [2] and [5] cannot both be applicable. So the applicable statements are one or more of the following:

    A. [1], [4], and [5]
    B. [1], [3], and [5]
    C. [1], [4], and [6]
    D. [1], [3], and [6]
    E. [2], [4], and [6]
    F. [2], [3], and [6]

If A applies then from conclusion [1] the killer was a man, from conclusion [4] the victim was a woman, and from premise [5] the killer and the victim were the same sex. This situation is impossible; so A does not apply.

If B applies then from the premises the killer and the victim were related, had the same occupation, and were the same sex. This situation contradicts the make-up of each family; so B does not apply.

If C applies then from the conclusions the killer was a man, and the victim was a female doctor. Then from premises [1] and [4] the killer was a lawyer, and the killer and the victim were related. This situation contradicts the make-up of each family; so C does not apply.

If D applies then from conclusion [1] the killer was a man, from conclusion [3] the victim was a man, and from premise [6] the killer and the victim were different sexes. This situation is impossible; so D does not apply.

If E applies then from conclusion [2] the killer was a doctor, from conclusion [6] the victim was a doctor, and from premise [4] the killer and the victim had different occupations. This situation is impossible; so E does not apply.

So F applies. From the conclusions the killer was a doctor, and the victim was a male doctor. Then from premise [6] the killer was a woman. Then from the family make-ups *the killer must be Betty*. Premise [2] reveals the victim is Duane, while premise [3] is consistent with conclusions [2] and [6].

39 / No Spade Played

Four tricks were played; so, from [4] and [5], the trump suit was led and won by the same player. Then, from [2] and [3], the sequence of leads and wins was either:

	I		II
X leads, wins		X leads	Y wins
X leads	Y wins		Y leads, wins
	Y leads, wins	X wins	Y leads
X wins	Y leads	X leads, wins	

Each win made by a player when not on lead indicates he or she played a trump. So each of the above sequences requires that one player have two trumps and the other player have one trump. Then, from [1], spades was trump.

If I is the correct sequence: spades, the trump suit, was not led and won by player X at the first trick—from [1], [5], and the fact that player Y must have held a spade at that point; spades was not led and won by player Y at the third trick—from [1], [5], and the fact that player X must have played a spade at the fourth trick.

So II is the correct sequence. Then spades was not led and won by player Y at the second trick—from [1], [5], and the fact that player X must have held a spade at that point. So spades was led and won by player X at the fourth trick.

From previous reasoning, a spade was played at the first, third, and fourth tricks. *So no spade was played at the second trick.*

To complete the details of the play: player X had to have led at the first trick a suit not held by player Y. Since this player had two spades, the man led a club at the first trick, from [1]. Then the man played a heart at the second trick, from [1]. So the woman led and won a diamond at the second trick, from [1] and [5]; she led a heart at the third trick, from [4]; and she played a diamond at the fourth trick, from [1].

40 / The Extortionist

Trial and error, using [3] and [4], reveals that the men and women sat around the table in one of the following arrangements (M represents man and W represents woman):

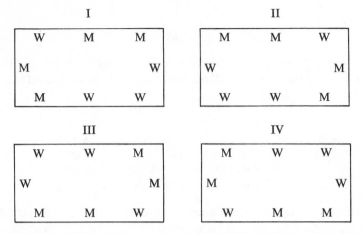

Then, from [2] and [6], arrangements II and IV are eliminated and the partial seating arrangement must be one of the following:

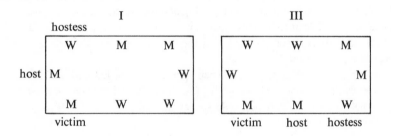

Then, from [1] and [5], arrangement I is eliminated and the partial seating arrangement must be the following (curved lines indicate the married couples):

III

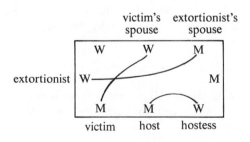

Then, from [7], Blair must be the extortionist's spouse; *so Blanche was the extortionist.* The complete seating arrangement is shown below.

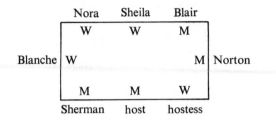

41 / The Unplaced Digits

From [1],

$$(A + B + C + D) + (D + E + F + G) + (G + H + I + A)$$
$$= 14 + 14 + 14 \text{ or}$$
$$2A + 2D + 2G + B + C + E + F + H + I = 42.$$

The sum of the ten digits is 45; so, if J represents an unplaced digit,

$$A + B + C + D + E + F + G + H + I = 45 - J.$$

Subtracting the second equation from the first equation, one gets:

$$A + D + G = J - 3.$$

Since $A + D + G$ must equal at least 3 and since J is at most 9, only the following values are possible:

	$A + D + G$	J
(i)	3	6
(ii)	4	7
(iii)	5	8
(iv)	6	9

Then one of the following must occur:

Then one gets:

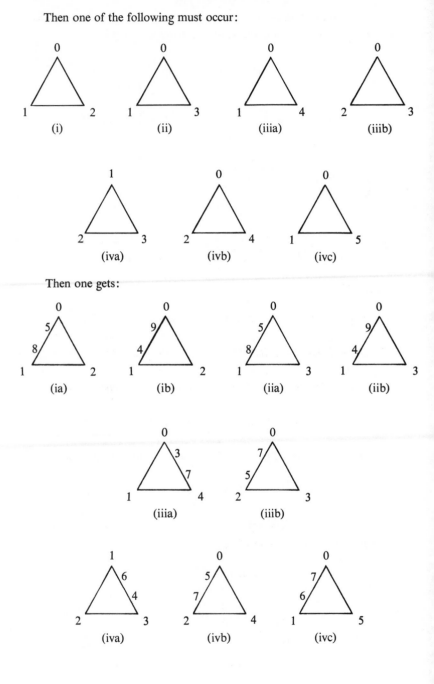

From this point, it is possible only to complete (i) and (ii) so that no digit is repeated.

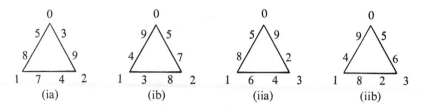

(ia)   (ib)   (iia)   (iib)

So, from [2], *6 and 7 were the unplaced digits.*

42 / Identified as the Criminal

From [1], the tall men were standing in one of the following arrangements (*t* represents tall man):

$$t\,t\,t\,t \quad \text{or} \quad t\,t\,t\,\_ \quad \text{or} \quad \_\,t\,t\,t \quad \text{or} \quad \_\,t\,t\,\_$$

From [2], the fair men were standing in one of the following arrangements (*f* represents fair man):

$$f\,f\,\_\,\_ \quad \text{or} \quad \_\,\_\,f\,f \quad \text{or} \quad f\,\_\,f\,f \quad \text{or} \quad f\,f\,\_\,f$$

From [3], the skinny men were standing in one of the following arrangements (*s* represents skinny man):

$$s\,\_\,\_\,s \quad \text{or} \quad s\,\_\,s\,\_ \quad \text{or} \quad \_\,s\,\_\,s \quad \text{or} \quad \_\,s\,\_\,\_ \quad \text{or} \quad \_\,\_\,s\,\_$$

From [4], the good-looking man was standing in one of the following positions (*g* represents good-looking man):

$$g\,\_\,\_\,\_ \quad \text{or} \quad \_\,\_\,\_\,g$$

From [5] and from the arrangements from [1], some of the above characteristics can be assigned as follows:

FIRST MAN	SECOND MAN	THIRD MAN	FOURTH MAN
fair	skinny	tall	good-looking
	tall		

Then, from the arrangements from [2], the partial records of character-istics must be one of the following:

	FIRST MAN	SECOND MAN	THIRD MAN	FOURTH MAN
I	fair	skinny tall fair	tall	good-looking
II	fair	skinny tall fair	tall	good-looking fair
III	fair	skinny tall	tall fair	good-looking fair

Then, from the arrangements from [3] and from [6], the fourth man may also be skinny in only I and III; no other man can be skinny in I, II, and III. Then, from the arrangements from [1] and from [6], the fourth man may also be tall in only I and only if the fourth man is not skinny; no other man can be tall in I, II, and III. Then from the arrangements from [4], no other man can be good-looking.

So the complete record of characteristics must be one of the following:

	FIRST MAN	SECOND MAN	THIRD MAN	FOURTH MAN
Ia	fair	skinny tall fair	tall	good-looking
Ib	fair	skinny tall fair	tall	good-looking skinny
Ic	fair	skinny tall fair	tall	good-looking tall
II	fair	skinny tall fair	tall	good-looking fair
IIIa	fair	skinny tall	tall fair	good-looking fair
IIIb	fair	skinny tall	tall fair	good-looking fair skinny

Records Ia, Ib, Ic, and II are eliminated from [7]. Records IIIa and IIIb reveal that *the witness identified the first man as the criminal.*

43 / The Last to Row across Limpid Lake

Four forward crossings were required for the eight persons to cross the lake in a boat that held only three persons; from [5], the boat contained only two persons during one of these crossings.

From [2], [3], and [5], a man must have been on the original shore until the last crossing (not necessarily the same man all of the time).

From the reasoning above and from [1], [4], and [5], the first four crossings were accomplished in one of the following ways (W represents woman, M represents man, a represents Abraham, b represents Barrett, c represents Clinton, and d represents Douglas):

I.   (i) M_cWWWW $M_aM_bM_d$ $\rightarrow$
     (ii) M_cWWWW $\leftarrow M_b$ M_aM_d
     (iii) M_bWW M_cWW $\rightarrow M_aM_d$
     (iv) M_bWW $\leftarrow M_d$ M_aM_cWW

II. (i) M_cM_dWWWW M_aM_b $\rightarrow$
     (ii) M_cM_dWWWW $\leftarrow M_b$ M_a
     (iii) M_bWWW M_cM_dW $\rightarrow M_a$
     (iv) M_bWWW $\leftarrow M_d$ M_aM_cW

Then, from [2], [3], and [5], Barrett rowed with two women during crossing (v); because this situation can occur only in way I, way II is eliminated. Then, from [2], [3], and [5], Abraham or Clinton rowed alone during return crossing (vi) and **Douglas rowed last** with him during crossing (vii).

44 / Card Number Six

Suppose card number six were an Ace. (a) Then neither cards number seven nor eight could be an Ace, from [5]; could be a Queen, from [4]; could be a King, from [2]. (b) Then at most one card of cards number seven and eight could be a Jack, from [3]. So, from [6], card number six is not an Ace.

Suppose card number six were a Queen. (a) Then none of cards number four, five, seven, and eight could be a Queen, from [5]; or could be an Ace, from [4]. (b) Then, from [6], two Aces and a Queen would be cards number one, two, and three; which, from [4] and [5], is impossible. So, from [6], card number six is not a Queen.

Suppose card number six were a Jack. (a) Then neither cards number seven nor eight could be an Ace, from [1]; could be a Jack, from [5];

could be a King, from [2]. (b) Then at most one card of cards number seven and eight could be a Queen, from [2]. So, from [6], card number six is not a Jack.

Then card number six is a King.

It is possible to determine cards number one through six. Since card number six is a King, card number five or four is a Queen, from [2] and [3]. If card number five is a Queen, then card number three is a Jack, from [3]. Then card number two is not a Queen, from [2], and cards number one and four are a King and a Queen, respectively, from [2]. Then, from [6], card number two must be a Jack, which contradicts [5]. So card number five is not a Queen and card number four is a Queen. Then neither of cards number one and three is a Queen, from [5]; neither of cards number seven and eight is a Queen, from [3]; and card number five is not a Queen, from previous reasoning. So card number two is a Queen. Then card number three is a Jack, from [3]; card number one is a King, from [2]. Then card number five is an Ace, from [5] and [6]. A Jack and an Ace are left for cards number seven and eight.

45 / The Shortest Time

From [2], each of the four men had a motor boat with a rate of speed in miles per hour equal to the man's distance in miles from Osborn's camp. Let d equal the distance in miles, r equal the rate of each boat in miles per hour, and t equal the time in hours for the second part of each trip. From [3], let c equal the current in miles per hour. Going upstream: $d/(r - c) = r/(r - c) = t$. Going downstream: $d/(r + c) = r/(r + c) = t$.

Then, from (1) and (4), the chart below represents the time for each part of each man's trip.

	TIME FOR FIRST PART IN HOURS	TIME FOR SECOND PART IN HOURS
Wilson	$r/(r - c) = 5/4$	$r/(r + c) = t$
Xavier	$r/(r - c) = 7/6$	$r/(r + c) = t$
Yeoman	$r/(r + c) = 5/6$	$r/(r - c) = t$
Zenger	$r/(r + c) = 3/4$	$r/(r - c) = t$

NOTE: *The r's and t's are different for each man, but the c's are the same for each man.*

For Wilson, $r = 5c$ and $t = 5/6$ or 50 minutes. For Xavier, $r = 7c$ and $t = 7/8$ or $52\frac{1}{2}$ minutes. For Yeoman, $r = 5c$ and $t = 5/4$ or 75 minutes. For Zenger, $r = 3c$ and $t = 3/2$ or 90 minutes.

Then the total time for Wilson is 125 minutes, the total time for Xavier is $122\frac{1}{2}$ minutes, the total time for Yeoman is 125 minutes, and the total time for Zenger is 135 minutes.

So Xavier made the round trip in the shortest time.

It turns out that Yeoman's camp is further upstream than Zenger's camp because Yeoman's distance is equal to $5c$ while Zenger's distance is equal to $3c$. Since Xavier's distance downstream is $7c$ and Wilson's distance downstream is $5c$, it turns out—perhaps, surprisingly—that Xavier's camp is the farthest from Osborn's camp.

46 / An Extraordinarily Empathic Man

Each man has exactly three characteristics. So, from [1] and [2], Adam has one of the following sets of characteristics:

> witty, handsome, strong
> witty, handsome, empathic
> handsome, strong, empathic
> strong, intelligent, empathic

So, from [1] and [3], Brad has one of the following sets of characteristics:

> witty, intelligent, handsome
> intelligent, handsome, strong
> intelligent, handsome, empathic
> handsome, strong, empathic

So, from [1] and [4], Cole has one of the following sets of characteristics:

> handsome, strong, intelligent
> handsome, strong, empathic
> strong, intelligent, empathic
> intelligent, witty, empathic

From the above sets of characteristics and from [1], if Adam is empathic then Brad and Cole are both intelligent and handsome; then Adam cannot be intelligent or handsome. This situation is impossible, so Adam is not empathic.

From the above sets of characteristics and from [1], if Brad is empathic then Adam and Cole are both handsome; then Brad cannot be handsome. This situation is impossible, so Brad is not empathic.

Then Cole must be empathic.

It is possible to find the three characteristics of only one man, and two characteristics of each of the other men. Since Cole is empathic: Adam is witty, handsome, and strong; Brad is handsome and intelligent; and, since Cole cannot be handsome, Cole is intelligent as well as empathic.

47 | Old Maid

From [1], the following situation must exist (A, B, and C represent one of a pair, while M represents the Old Maid):

DOROTHY'S HAND	LORETTA'S HAND	ROSALYN'S HAND
A	$B\ C$	$A\ B\ C\ M$

Then, from [2], [3], and [4], the drawings proceeded in any of the following orders:

	(a)			(b)			(c)	
A	$ABCM$	BC	A	$ABCM$	BC	A	BC	$ABCM$
AB	ACM	BC	AM	ABC	BC	AB	C	$ABCM$
AB	$AM\cancel{CC}$	B	AM	$AB\cancel{CC}$	B	AB	CA	BCM
B	AM	AB	M	AB	AB			
BM	A	AB	MB	A	AB			
BM	AB	A						

	(d)			(e)			(f)	
A	BC	$ABCM$	A	BC	$ABCM$	A	BC	$ABCM$
AB	C	$ABCM$	AB	C	$ABCM$	AB	C	$ABCM$
AB	CM	ABC	AB	$\cancel{CC}$	ABM	AB	$\cancel{CC}$	ABM
B	CM	$\cancel{AA}BC$	B	$-$	$\cancel{AA}BM$	B	$-$	$\cancel{AA}BM$
BC	M	BC	$\cancel{BB}$	$-$	M	BM	$-$	B
BC	MB	C				M	$-$	$\cancel{BB}$

Orders (a), (b), (c), and (d) cannot be completed, from [4]; so these orders are eliminated.

From [5], order (e) is eliminated.

So order (f) is the correct order, and *Dorothy was left with the Old Maid*.

48 / The Smiths

From [1], Audrey does calisthenics on either Sunday and Friday or Monday and Saturday.

    I. If Audrey does calisthenics on Sunday and Friday then, from [2] and [5], Brenda does calisthenics on Tuesday and Saturday.

    II. If Audrey does calisthenics on Monday and Saturday then, from [2] and [5], Brenda does calisthenics on Sunday and Thursday.

If I is correct then, from [5], either Conrad or Daniel does calisthenics on Monday, Wednesday, or Thursday; in which case, from [3] and [4],

    Ia. Conrad does calisthenics on Monday and Thursday and Daniel does calisthenics on Wednesday or

    Ib. Daniel does calisthenics on Monday and Wednesday and Conrad does calisthenics on Thursday.

If II is correct then, from [5], either Conrad or Daniel does calisthenics on Tuesday, Wednesday, or Friday; in which case, from [3] and [4],

    IIa. Conrad does calisthenics on Tuesday and Friday and Daniel does calisthenics on Wednesday or

    IIb. Daniel does calisthenics on Wednesday and Friday and Conrad does calisthenics on Tuesday.

The above conclusions may be put into chart form as follows:

	AUDREY	BRENDA	CONRAD	DANIEL
Ia	Sun, Fri	Tues, Sat	Mon, Thurs	Wed,
Ib	Sun, Fri	Tues, Sat	Thurs,	Mon, Wed
IIa	Mon, Sat	Sun, Thurs	Tues, Fri	Wed,
IIb	Mon, Sat	Sun, Thurs	Tues,	Wed, Fri

From [3] and [5], no additional day is possible for Conrad in Ib and IIb. From [4] and [5], Friday is possible for Daniel in Ia, and Monday is possible for Daniel in IIa. In any case, *the Smiths are Audrey and Daniel.*

49 | The Hired Man

In the charts below, A represents Alden, B represents Brent, C represents Craig, D represents Derek, *g* represents high school graduate, *w* represents at least two years of previous work, *v* represents veteran, *r* represents satisfactory references, X represents meets the requirement, and O represents does not meet the requirement. The first chart shows the result of using [4] and [5].

	A	B	C	D
g				
w				
v		X	X	
r				X

Then, from [2] and [3], one of four partially filled charts is possible.

I

	A	B	C	D
g	X	X		
w			X	X
v		X	X	
r				X

II

	A	B	C	D
g	X	X		
w			O	O
v		X	X	
r				X

III

	A	B	C	D
g	O	O		
w			X	X
v		X	X	
r				X

IV

	A	B	C	D
g	O	O		
w			O	O
v		X	X	
r				X

In IV, no one can meet both the *g* and *w* requirements; so, from [1], chart IV is eliminated.

From [1], O's can be added to each of charts I, II, and III.

	I			
	A	B	C	D
g	X	X	O	
w		O	X	X
v	O	X	X	O
r			O	X

	II			
	A	B	C	D
g	X	X		
w			O	O
v	O	X	X	
r				X

	III			
	A	B	C	D
g	O	O		
w		O	X	X
v		X	X	O
r			O	X

From [1] again, an X can be added to each of charts I, II, and III.

	I			
	A	B	C	D
g	X	X	O	
w		O	X	X
v	O	X	X	O
r		X	O	X

	II			
	A	B	C	D
g	X	X		
w		X	O	O
v	O	X	X	
r				X

	III			
	A	B	C	D
g	O	O		X
w		O	X	X
v		X	X	O
r			O	X

From [1] again, O's can be added to each of charts I, II, and III.

	I			
	A	B	C	D
g	X	X	O	O
w		O	X	X
v	O	X	X	O
r	O	X	O	X

	II			
	A	B	C	D
g	X	X	O	
w	O	X	O	O
v	O	X	X	
r				X

	III			
	A	B	C	D
g	O	O	O	X
w		O	X	X
v		X	X	O
r			O	X

Chart III is now eliminated, from [1], because no one can meet both the g and v requirements. At this point only Brent can meet more requirements than each of the other men; so **Brent was hired.**

Charts I and II may be completed as follows. From [1], X's can be added to each of charts I and II.

	I			
	A	B	C	D
g	X	X	O	O
w	X	O	X	X
v	O	X	X	O
r	O	X	O	X

	II			
	A	B	C	D
g	X	X	O	
w	O	X	O	O
v	O	X	X	
r		X		X

Then chart II can be completed only by adding O's.

50 / More Types of Crime

From [1], the murderers were seated in one of the following arrangements (*m* represents murderer):

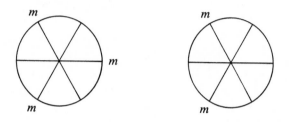

From [2], the extortionists were seated in one of the following arrangements (*e* represents extortionist):

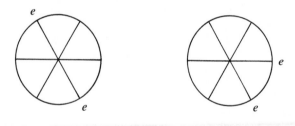

From [3], the swindlers were seated in one of the following arrangements (*s* represents swindler):

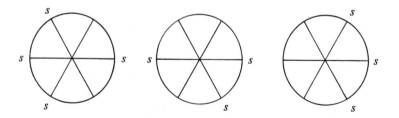

From [4], the thieves were seated in one of the following arrangements (*t* represents thief):

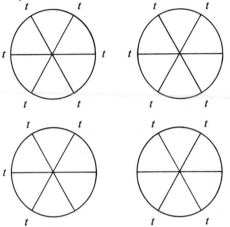

If one person committed four types of crime, each of the other persons could not have committed more than one type of crime, from [5]. But from the above arrangements, there were at least two murderers, two extortionists, three swindlers, and four thieves at the table. So no one committed four types of crime. Similarly, one person could not have committed two types of crime while each of the other persons committed only one type of crime.

So, from [6], the maximum number of types of crime committed by one person was three. Then, from the above arrangements, one person committed just three types of crime, each of three persons committed just two types of crime, and each of two persons committed just one type of crime. So there were exactly two murderers, two extortionists, three swindlers, and four thieves.

From [8] and [9], then, some types of crime can be incorporated into the seating arrangement as follows:

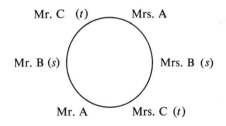

Then, from the possible arrangements derived from [3] and from [10], the situation becomes either:

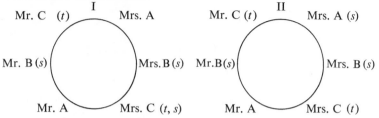

From the possible arrangements derived from [4] and from [5] and [7], situation I is impossible and situation II becomes:

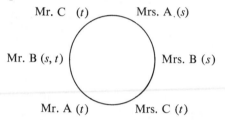

Then, from the possible arrangements derived from [2] and from [5] and [7], situation II becomes:

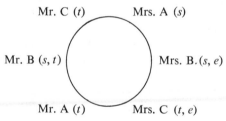

Then, from the possible arrangements derived from [1] and from [5] and [7], situation II becomes:

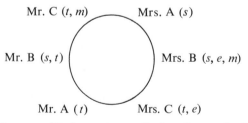

So Mrs. Brice committed more types of crime than each of the other persons.

A CATALOG OF SELECTED
DOVER BOOKS
IN ALL FIELDS OF INTEREST

A CATALOG OF SELECTED DOVER
BOOKS IN ALL FIELDS OF INTEREST

CONCERNING THE SPIRITUAL IN ART, Wassily Kandinsky. Pioneering work by father of abstract art. Thoughts on color theory, nature of art. Analysis of earlier masters. 12 illustrations. 80pp. of text. 5⅜ x 8½. 23411-8 Pa. $4.95

ANIMALS: 1,419 Copyright-Free Illustrations of Mammals, Birds, Fish, Insects, etc., Jim Harter (ed.). Clear wood engravings present, in extremely lifelike poses, over 1,000 species of animals. One of the most extensive pictorial sourcebooks of its kind. Captions. Index. 284pp. 9 x 12. 23766-4 Pa. $14.95

CELTIC ART: The Methods of Construction, George Bain. Simple geometric techniques for making Celtic interlacements, spirals, Kells-type initials, animals, humans, etc. Over 500 illustrations. 160pp. 9 x 12. (Available in U.S. only.) 22923-8 Pa. $9.95

AN ATLAS OF ANATOMY FOR ARTISTS, Fritz Schider. Most thorough reference work on art anatomy in the world. Hundreds of illustrations, including selections from works by Vesalius, Leonardo, Goya, Ingres, Michelangelo, others. 593 illustrations. 192pp. 7⅛ x 10¼. 20241-0 Pa. $9.95

CELTIC HAND STROKE-BY-STROKE (Irish Half-Uncial from "The Book of Kells"): An Arthur Baker Calligraphy Manual, Arthur Baker. Complete guide to creating each letter of the alphabet in distinctive Celtic manner. Covers hand position, strokes, pens, inks, paper, more. Illustrated. 48pp. 8¼ x 11. 24336-2 Pa. $3.95

EASY ORIGAMI, John Montroll. Charming collection of 32 projects (hat, cup, pelican, piano, swan, many more) specially designed for the novice origami hobbyist. Clearly illustrated easy-to-follow instructions insure that even beginning papercrafters will achieve successful results. 48pp. 8¼ x 11. 27298-2 Pa. $3.50

THE COMPLETE BOOK OF BIRDHOUSE CONSTRUCTION FOR WOODWORKERS, Scott D. Campbell. Detailed instructions, illustrations, tables. Also data on bird habitat and instinct patterns. Bibliography. 3 tables. 63 illustrations in 15 figures. 48pp. 5¼ x 8½. 24407-5 Pa. $2.50

BLOOMINGDALE'S ILLUSTRATED 1886 CATALOG: Fashions, Dry Goods and Housewares, Bloomingdale Brothers. Famed merchants' extremely rare catalog depicting about 1,700 products: clothing, housewares, firearms, dry goods, jewelry, more. Invaluable for dating, identifying vintage items. Also, copyright-free graphics for artists, designers. Co-published with Henry Ford Museum & Greenfield Village. 160pp. 8¼ x 11. 25780-0 Pa. $10.95

HISTORIC COSTUME IN PICTURES, Braun & Schneider. Over 1,450 costumed figures in clearly detailed engravings–from dawn of civilization to end of 19th century. Captions. Many folk costumes. 256pp. 8⅜ x 11¾. 23150-X Pa. $12.95

STICKLEY CRAFTSMAN FURNITURE CATALOGS, Gustav Stickley and L. & J. G. Stickley. Beautiful, functional furniture in two authentic catalogs from 1910. 594 illustrations, including 277 photos, show settles, rockers, armchairs, reclining chairs, bookcases, desks, tables. 183pp. 6½ x 9¼. 23838-5 Pa. $11.95

AMERICAN LOCOMOTIVES IN HISTORIC PHOTOGRAPHS: 1858 to 1949, Ron Ziel (ed.). A rare collection of 126 meticulously detailed official photographs, called "builder portraits," of American locomotives that majestically chronicle the rise of steam locomotive power in America. Introduction. Detailed captions. xi+ 129pp. 9 x 12. 27393-8 Pa. $13.95

AMERICA'S LIGHTHOUSES: An Illustrated History, Francis Ross Holland, Jr. Delightfully written, profusely illustrated fact-filled survey of over 200 American lighthouses since 1716. History, anecdotes, technological advances, more. 240pp. 8 x 10¾. 25576-X Pa. $12.95

TOWARDS A NEW ARCHITECTURE, Le Corbusier. Pioneering manifesto by founder of "International School." Technical and aesthetic theories, views of industry, economics, relation of form to function, "mass-production split" and much more. Profusely illustrated. 320pp. 6⅛ x 9¼. (Available in U.S. only.) 25023-7 Pa. $9.95

HOW THE OTHER HALF LIVES, Jacob Riis. Famous journalistic record, exposing poverty and degradation of New York slums around 1900, by major social reformer. 100 striking and influential photographs. 233pp. 10 x 7⅞. 22012-5 Pa. $11.95

FRUIT KEY AND TWIG KEY TO TREES AND SHRUBS, William M. Harlow. One of the handiest and most widely used identification aids. Fruit key covers 120 deciduous and evergreen species; twig key 160 deciduous species. Easily used. Over 300 photographs. 126pp. 5⅜ x 8½. 20511-8 Pa. $3.95

COMMON BIRD SONGS, Dr. Donald J. Borror. Songs of 60 most common U.S. birds: robins, sparrows, cardinals, bluejays, finches, more–arranged in order of increasing complexity. Up to 9 variations of songs of each species. Cassette and manual 99911-4 $8.95

ORCHIDS AS HOUSE PLANTS, Rebecca Tyson Northen. Grow cattleyas and many other kinds of orchids–in a window, in a case, or under artificial light. 63 illustrations. 148pp. 5⅜ x 8½. 23261-1 Pa. $5.95

MONSTER MAZES, Dave Phillips. Masterful mazes at four levels of difficulty. Avoid deadly perils and evil creatures to find magical treasures. Solutions for all 32 exciting illustrated puzzles. 48pp. 8¼ x 11. 26005-4 Pa. $2.95

MOZART'S DON GIOVANNI (DOVER OPERA LIBRETTO SERIES), Wolfgang Amadeus Mozart. Introduced and translated by Ellen H. Bleiler. Standard Italian libretto, with complete English translation. Convenient and thoroughly portable–an ideal companion for reading along with a recording or the performance itself. Introduction. List of characters. Plot summary. 121pp. 5¼ x 8½. 24944-1 Pa. $3.95

TECHNICAL MANUAL AND DICTIONARY OF CLASSICAL BALLET, Gail Grant. Defines, explains, comments on steps, movements, poses and concepts. 15-page pictorial section. Basic book for student, viewer. 127pp. 5⅜ x 8½. 21843-0 Pa. $4.95

THE CLARINET AND CLARINET PLAYING, David Pino. Lively, comprehensive work features suggestions about technique, musicianship, and musical interpretation, as well as guidelines for teaching, making your own reeds, and preparing for public performance. Includes an intriguing look at clarinet history. "A godsend," *The Clarinet*, Journal of the International Clarinet Society. Appendixes. 7 illus. 320pp. 5⅜ x 8½. 40270-3 Pa. $9.95

HOLLYWOOD GLAMOR PORTRAITS, John Kobal (ed.). 145 photos from 1926-49. Harlow, Gable, Bogart, Bacall; 94 stars in all. Full background on photographers, technical aspects. 160pp. 8⅜ x 11¼. 23352-9 Pa. $12.95

THE ANNOTATED CASEY AT THE BAT: A Collection of Ballads about the Mighty Casey/Third, Revised Edition, Martin Gardner (ed.). Amusing sequels and parodies of one of America's best-loved poems: Casey's Revenge, Why Casey Whiffed, Casey's Sister at the Bat, others. 256pp. 5⅜ x 8½. 28598-7 Pa. $8.95

THE RAVEN AND OTHER FAVORITE POEMS, Edgar Allan Poe. Over 40 of the author's most memorable poems: "The Bells," "Ulalume," "Israfel," "To Helen," "The Conqueror Worm," "Eldorado," "Annabel Lee," many more. Alphabetic lists of titles and first lines. 64pp. 5³⁄₁₆ x 8¼. 26685-0 Pa. $1.00

PERSONAL MEMOIRS OF U. S. GRANT, Ulysses Simpson Grant. Intelligent, deeply moving firsthand account of Civil War campaigns, considered by many the finest military memoirs ever written. Includes letters, historic photographs, maps and more. 528pp. 6⅛ x 9¼. 28587-1 Pa. $12.95

ANCIENT EGYPTIAN MATERIALS AND INDUSTRIES, A. Lucas and J. Harris. Fascinating, comprehensive, thoroughly documented text describes this ancient civilization's vast resources and the processes that incorporated them in daily life, including the use of animal products, building materials, cosmetics, perfumes and incense, fibers, glazed ware, glass and its manufacture, materials used in the mummification process, and much more. 544pp. 6⅛ x 9¼. (Available in U.S. only.) 40446-3 Pa. $16.95

RUSSIAN STORIES/РУССКИЕ РАССКАЗЫ: A Dual-Language Book, edited by Gleb Struve. Twelve tales by such masters as Chekhov, Tolstoy, Dostoevsky, Pushkin, others. Excellent word-for-word English translations on facing pages, plus teaching and study aids, Russian/English vocabulary, biographical/critical introductions, more. 416pp. 5⅜ x 8½. 26244-8 Pa. $9.95

PHILADELPHIA THEN AND NOW: 60 Sites Photographed in the Past and Present, Kenneth Finkel and Susan Oyama. Rare photographs of City Hall, Logan Square, Independence Hall, Betsy Ross House, other landmarks juxtaposed with contemporary views. Captures changing face of historic city. Introduction. Captions. 128pp. 8¼ x 11. 25790-8 Pa. $9.95

AIA ARCHITECTURAL GUIDE TO NASSAU AND SUFFOLK COUNTIES, LONG ISLAND, The American Institute of Architects, Long Island Chapter, and the Society for the Preservation of Long Island Antiquities. Comprehensive, well-researched and generously illustrated volume brings to life over three centuries of Long Island's great architectural heritage. More than 240 photographs with authoritative, extensively detailed captions. 176pp. 8¼ x 11. 26946-9 Pa. $14.95

NORTH AMERICAN INDIAN LIFE: Customs and Traditions of 23 Tribes, Elsie Clews Parsons (ed.). 27 fictionalized essays by noted anthropologists examine religion, customs, government, additional facets of life among the Winnebago, Crow, Zuni, Eskimo, other tribes. 480pp. 6⅛ x 9¼. 27377-6 Pa. $10.95

FRANK LLOYD WRIGHT'S DANA HOUSE, Donald Hoffmann. Pictorial essay of residential masterpiece with over 160 interior and exterior photos, plans, elevations, sketches and studies. 128pp. 9¼ x 10¾. 29120-0 Pa. $12.95

THE MALE AND FEMALE FIGURE IN MOTION: 60 Classic Photographic Sequences, Eadweard Muybridge. 60 true-action photographs of men and women walking, running, climbing, bending, turning, etc., reproduced from rare 19th-century masterpiece. vi + 121pp. 9 x 12. 24745-7 Pa. $12.95

1001 QUESTIONS ANSWERED ABOUT THE SEASHORE, N. J. Berrill and Jacquelyn Berrill. Queries answered about dolphins, sea snails, sponges, starfish, fishes, shore birds, many others. Covers appearance, breeding, growth, feeding, much more. 305pp. 5¼ x 8¼. 23366-9 Pa. $9.95

ATTRACTING BIRDS TO YOUR YARD, William J. Weber. Easy-to-follow guide offers advice on how to attract the greatest diversity of birds: birdhouses, feeders, water and waterers, much more. 96pp. 5³⁄₁₆ x 8¼. 28927-3 Pa. $2.50

MEDICINAL AND OTHER USES OF NORTH AMERICAN PLANTS: A Historical Survey with Special Reference to the Eastern Indian Tribes, Charlotte Erichsen-Brown. Chronological historical citations document 500 years of usage of plants, trees, shrubs native to eastern Canada, northeastern U.S. Also complete identifying information. 343 illustrations. 544pp. 6½ x 9¼. 25951-X Pa. $12.95

STORYBOOK MAZES, Dave Phillips. 23 stories and mazes on two-page spreads: Wizard of Oz, Treasure Island, Robin Hood, etc. Solutions. 64pp. 8¼ x 11.
23628-5 Pa. $2.95

AMERICAN NEGRO SONGS: 230 Folk Songs and Spirituals, Religious and Secular, John W. Work. This authoritative study traces the African influences of songs sung and played by black Americans at work, in church, and as entertainment. The author discusses the lyric significance of such songs as "Swing Low, Sweet Chariot," "John Henry," and others and offers the words and music for 230 songs. Bibliography. Index of Song Titles. 272pp. 6½ x 9¼. 40271-1 Pa. $9.95

MOVIE-STAR PORTRAITS OF THE FORTIES, John Kobal (ed.). 163 glamor, studio photos of 106 stars of the 1940s: Rita Hayworth, Ava Gardner, Marlon Brando, Clark Gable, many more. 176pp. 8⅜ x 11¼. 23546-7 Pa. $14.95

BENCHLEY LOST AND FOUND, Robert Benchley. Finest humor from early 30s, about pet peeves, child psychologists, post office and others. Mostly unavailable elsewhere. 73 illustrations by Peter Arno and others. 183pp. 5⅜ x 8½. 22410-4 Pa. $6.95

YEKL and THE IMPORTED BRIDEGROOM AND OTHER STORIES OF YIDDISH NEW YORK, Abraham Cahan. Film Hester Street based on *Yekl* (1896). Novel, other stories among first about Jewish immigrants on N.Y.'s East Side. 240pp. 5⅜ x 8½. 22427-9 Pa. $7.95

SELECTED POEMS, Walt Whitman. Generous sampling from *Leaves of Grass*. Twenty-four poems include "I Hear America Singing," "Song of the Open Road," "I Sing the Body Electric," "When Lilacs Last in the Dooryard Bloom'd," "O Captain! My Captain!"—all reprinted from an authoritative edition. Lists of titles and first lines. 128pp. 5³⁄₁₆ x 8¼. 26878-0 Pa. $1.00

THE BEST TALES OF HOFFMANN, E. T. A. Hoffmann. 10 of Hoffmann's most important stories: "Nutcracker and the King of Mice," "The Golden Flowerpot," etc. 458pp. 5⅜ x 8½. 21793-0 Pa. $9.95

FROM FETISH TO GOD IN ANCIENT EGYPT, E. A. Wallis Budge. Rich detailed survey of Egyptian conception of "God" and gods, magic, cult of animals, Osiris, more. Also, superb English translations of hymns and legends. 240 illustrations. 545pp. 5⅜ x 8½. 25803-3 Pa. $13.95

FRENCH STORIES/CONTES FRANÇAIS: A Dual-Language Book, Wallace Fowlie. Ten stories by French masters, Voltaire to Camus: "Micromegas" by Voltaire; "The Atheist's Mass" by Balzac; "Minuet" by de Maupassant; "The Guest" by Camus, six more. Excellent English translations on facing pages. Also French-English vocabulary list, exercises, more. 352pp. 5⅜ x 8½. 26443-2 Pa. $9.95

CHICAGO AT THE TURN OF THE CENTURY IN PHOTOGRAPHS: 122 Historic Views from the Collections of the Chicago Historical Society, Larry A. Viskochil. Rare large-format prints offer detailed views of City Hall, State Street, the Loop, Hull House, Union Station, many other landmarks, circa 1904-1913. Introduction. Captions. Maps. 144pp. 9⅜ x 12¼. 24656-6 Pa. $12.95

OLD BROOKLYN IN EARLY PHOTOGRAPHS, 1865-1929, William Lee Younger. Luna Park, Gravesend race track, construction of Grand Army Plaza, moving of Hotel Brighton, etc. 157 previously unpublished photographs. 165pp. 8⅞ x 11¾. 23587-4 Pa. $13.95

THE MYTHS OF THE NORTH AMERICAN INDIANS, Lewis Spence. Rich anthology of the myths and legends of the Algonquins, Iroquois, Pawnees and Sioux, prefaced by an extensive historical and ethnological commentary. 36 illustrations. 480pp. 5⅜ x 8½. 25967-6 Pa. $10.95

AN ENCYCLOPEDIA OF BATTLES: Accounts of Over 1,560 Battles from 1479 B.C. to the Present, David Eggenberger. Essential details of every major battle in recorded history from the first battle of Megiddo in 1479 B.C. to Grenada in 1984. List of Battle Maps. New Appendix covering the years 1967-1984. Index. 99 illustrations. 544pp. 6½ x 9¼. 24913-1 Pa. $16.95

SAILING ALONE AROUND THE WORLD, Captain Joshua Slocum. First man to sail around the world, alone, in small boat. One of great feats of seamanship told in delightful manner. 67 illustrations. 294pp. 5⅜ x 8½. 20326-3 Pa. $6.95

ANARCHISM AND OTHER ESSAYS, Emma Goldman. Powerful, penetrating, prophetic essays on direct action, role of minorities, prison reform, puritan hypocrisy, violence, etc. 271pp. 5⅜ x 8½. 22484-8 Pa. $7.95

MYTHS OF THE HINDUS AND BUDDHISTS, Ananda K. Coomaraswamy and Sister Nivedita. Great stories of the epics; deeds of Krishna, Shiva, taken from puranas, Vedas, folk tales; etc. 32 illustrations. 400pp. 5⅜ x 8½. 21759-0 Pa. $12.95

THE TRAUMA OF BIRTH, Otto Rank. Rank's controversial thesis that anxiety neurosis is caused by profound psychological trauma which occurs at birth. 256pp. 5⅜ x 8½. 27974-X Pa. $7.95

A THEOLOGICO-POLITICAL TREATISE, Benedict Spinoza. Also contains unfinished Political Treatise. Great classic on religious liberty, theory of government on common consent. R. Elwes translation. Total of 421pp. 5⅜ x 8½. 20249-6 Pa. $10.95

MY BONDAGE AND MY FREEDOM, Frederick Douglass. Born a slave, Douglass became outspoken force in antislavery movement. The best of Douglass' autobiographies. Graphic description of slave life. 464pp. 5⅜ x 8½. 22457-0 Pa. $8.95

FOLLOWING THE EQUATOR: A Journey Around the World, Mark Twain. Fascinating humorous account of 1897 voyage to Hawaii, Australia, India, New Zealand, etc. Ironic, bemused reports on peoples, customs, climate, flora and fauna, politics, much more. 197 illustrations. 720pp. 5⅜ x 8½.   26113-1 Pa. $15.95

THE PEOPLE CALLED SHAKERS, Edward D. Andrews. Definitive study of Shakers: origins, beliefs, practices, dances, social organization, furniture and crafts, etc. 33 illustrations. 351pp. 5⅜ x 8½.   21081-2 Pa. $10.95

THE MYTHS OF GREECE AND ROME, H. A. Guerber. A classic of mythology, generously illustrated, long prized for its simple, graphic, accurate retelling of the principal myths of Greece and Rome, and for its commentary on their origins and significance. With 64 illustrations by Michelangelo, Raphael, Titian, Rubens, Canova, Bernini and others. 480pp. 5⅜ x 8½.   27584-1 Pa. $9.95

PSYCHOLOGY OF MUSIC, Carl E. Seashore. Classic work discusses music as a medium from psychological viewpoint. Clear treatment of physical acoustics, auditory apparatus, sound perception, development of musical skills, nature of musical feeling, host of other topics. 88 figures. 408pp. 5⅜ x 8½.   21851-1 Pa. $11.95

THE PHILOSOPHY OF HISTORY, Georg W. Hegel. Great classic of Western thought develops concept that history is not chance but rational process, the evolution of freedom. 457pp. 5⅜ x 8½.   20112-0 Pa. $9.95

THE BOOK OF TEA, Kakuzo Okakura. Minor classic of the Orient: entertaining, charming explanation, interpretation of traditional Japanese culture in terms of tea ceremony. 94pp. 5⅜ x 8½.   20070-1 Pa. $3.95

LIFE IN ANCIENT EGYPT, Adolf Erman. Fullest, most thorough, detailed older account with much not in more recent books, domestic life, religion, magic, medicine, commerce, much more. Many illustrations reproduce tomb paintings, carvings, hieroglyphs, etc. 597pp. 5⅜ x 8½.   22632-8 Pa. $12.95

SUNDIALS, Their Theory and Construction, Albert Waugh. Far and away the best, most thorough coverage of ideas, mathematics concerned, types, construction, adjusting anywhere. Simple, nontechnical treatment allows even children to build several of these dials. Over 100 illustrations. 230pp. 5⅜ x 8½.   22947-5 Pa. $8.95

THEORETICAL HYDRODYNAMICS, L. M. Milne-Thomson. Classic exposition of the mathematical theory of fluid motion, applicable to both hydrodynamics and aerodynamics. Over 600 exercises. 768pp. 6⅛ x 9¼.   68970-0 Pa. $20.95

SONGS OF EXPERIENCE: Facsimile Reproduction with 26 Plates in Full Color, William Blake. 26 full-color plates from a rare 1826 edition. Includes "TheTyger," "London," "Holy Thursday," and other poems. Printed text of poems. 48pp. 5¼ x 7.
24636-1 Pa. $4.95

OLD-TIME VIGNETTES IN FULL COLOR, Carol Belanger Grafton (ed.). Over 390 charming, often sentimental illustrations, selected from archives of Victorian graphics—pretty women posing, children playing, food, flowers, kittens and puppies, smiling cherubs, birds and butterflies, much more. All copyright-free. 48pp. 9¼ x 12¼.
27269-9 Pa. $7.95

PERSPECTIVE FOR ARTISTS, Rex Vicat Cole. Depth, perspective of sky and sea, shadows, much more, not usually covered. 391 diagrams, 81 reproductions of drawings and paintings. 279pp. 5⅜ x 8½. 22487-2 Pa. $9.95

DRAWING THE LIVING FIGURE, Joseph Sheppard. Innovative approach to artistic anatomy focuses on specifics of surface anatomy, rather than muscles and bones. Over 170 drawings of live models in front, back and side views, and in widely varying poses. Accompanying diagrams. 177 illustrations. Introduction. Index. 144pp. 8⅜ x11¼. 26723-7 Pa. $9.95

GOTHIC AND OLD ENGLISH ALPHABETS: 100 Complete Fonts, Dan X. Solo. Add power, elegance to posters, signs, other graphics with 100 stunning copyright-free alphabets: Blackstone, Dolbey, Germania, 97 more–including many lower-case, numerals, punctuation marks. 104pp. 8⅛ x 11. 24695-7 Pa. $8.95

HOW TO DO BEADWORK, Mary White. Fundamental book on craft from simple projects to five-bead chains and woven works. 106 illustrations. 142pp. 5⅜ x 8. 20697-1 Pa. $5.95

THE BOOK OF WOOD CARVING, Charles Marshall Sayers. Finest book for beginners discusses fundamentals and offers 34 designs. "Absolutely first rate . . . well thought out and well executed."–E. J. Tangerman. 118pp. 7¾ x 10⅝. 23654-4 Pa. $7.95

ILLUSTRATED CATALOG OF CIVIL WAR MILITARY GOODS: Union Army Weapons, Insignia, Uniform Accessories, and Other Equipment, Schuyler, Hartley, and Graham. Rare, profusely illustrated 1846 catalog includes Union Army uniform and dress regulations, arms and ammunition, coats, insignia, flags, swords, rifles, etc. 226 illustrations. 160pp. 9 x 12. 24939-5 Pa. $10.95

WOMEN'S FASHIONS OF THE EARLY 1900s: An Unabridged Republication of "New York Fashions, 1909," National Cloak & Suit Co. Rare catalog of mail-order fashions documents women's and children's clothing styles shortly after the turn of the century. Captions offer full descriptions, prices. Invaluable resource for fashion, costume historians. Approximately 725 illustrations. 128pp. 8⅜ x 11¼. 27276-1 Pa. $11.95

THE 1912 AND 1915 GUSTAV STICKLEY FURNITURE CATALOGS, Gustav Stickley. With over 200 detailed illustrations and descriptions, these two catalogs are essential reading and reference materials and identification guides for Stickley furniture. Captions cite materials, dimensions and prices. 112pp. 6½ x 9¼. 26676-1 Pa. $9.95

EARLY AMERICAN LOCOMOTIVES, John H. White, Jr. Finest locomotive engravings from early 19th century: historical (1804–74), main-line (after 1870), special, foreign, etc. 147 plates. 142pp. 11⅜ x 8¼. 22772-3 Pa. $12.95

THE TALL SHIPS OF TODAY IN PHOTOGRAPHS, Frank O. Braynard. Lavishly illustrated tribute to nearly 100 majestic contemporary sailing vessels: Amerigo Vespucci, Clearwater, Constitution, Eagle, Mayflower, Sea Cloud, Victory, many more. Authoritative captions provide statistics, background on each ship. 190 black-and-white photographs and illustrations. Introduction. 128pp. 8⅞ x 11¾. 27163-3 Pa. $14.95

LITTLE BOOK OF EARLY AMERICAN CRAFTS AND TRADES, Peter Stockham (ed.). 1807 children's book explains crafts and trades: baker, hatter, cooper, potter, and many others. 23 copperplate illustrations. 140pp. $4^{5}/_{8}$ x 6.
23336-7 Pa. $4.95

VICTORIAN FASHIONS AND COSTUMES FROM HARPER'S BAZAR, 1867–1898, Stella Blum (ed.). Day costumes, evening wear, sports clothes, shoes, hats, other accessories in over 1,000 detailed engravings. 320pp. 9⅜ x 12¼.
22990-4 Pa. $16.95

GUSTAV STICKLEY, THE CRAFTSMAN, Mary Ann Smith. Superb study surveys broad scope of Stickley's achievement, especially in architecture. Design philosophy, rise and fall of the Craftsman empire, descriptions and floor plans for many Craftsman houses, more. 86 black-and-white halftones. 31 line illustrations. Introduction 208pp. 6½ x 9¼.
27210-9 Pa. $9.95

THE LONG ISLAND RAIL ROAD IN EARLY PHOTOGRAPHS, Ron Ziel. Over 220 rare photos, informative text document origin (1844) and development of rail service on Long Island. Vintage views of early trains, locomotives, stations, passengers, crews, much more. Captions. 8⅞ x 11¾.
26301-0 Pa. $14.95

VOYAGE OF THE LIBERDADE, Joshua Slocum. Great 19th-century mariner's thrilling, first-hand account of the wreck of his ship off South America, the 35-foot boat he built from the wreckage, and its remarkable voyage home. 128pp. 5⅜ x 8½.
40022-0 Pa. $5.95

TEN BOOKS ON ARCHITECTURE, Vitruvius. The most important book ever written on architecture. Early Roman aesthetics, technology, classical orders, site selection, all other aspects. Morgan translation. 331pp. 5⅜ x 8½. 20645-9 Pa. $8.95

THE HUMAN FIGURE IN MOTION, Eadweard Muybridge. More than 4,500 stopped-action photos, in action series, showing undraped men, women, children jumping, lying down, throwing, sitting, wrestling, carrying, etc. 390pp. 7⅞ x 10⅝.
20204-6 Clothbd. $27.95

TREES OF THE EASTERN AND CENTRAL UNITED STATES AND CANADA, William M. Harlow. Best one-volume guide to 140 trees. Full descriptions, woodlore, range, etc. Over 600 illustrations. Handy size. 288pp. 4½ x 6⅜.
20395-6 Pa. $6.95

SONGS OF WESTERN BIRDS, Dr. Donald J. Borror. Complete song and call repertoire of 60 western species, including flycatchers, juncoes, cactus wrens, many more—includes fully illustrated booklet.   Cassette and manual 99913-0 $8.95

GROWING AND USING HERBS AND SPICES, Milo Miloradovich. Versatile handbook provides all the information needed for cultivation and use of all the herbs and spices available in North America. 4 illustrations. Index. Glossary. 236pp. 5⅜ x 8½.
25058-X Pa. $7.95

BIG BOOK OF MAZES AND LABYRINTHS, Walter Shepherd. 50 mazes and labyrinths in all—classical, solid, ripple, and more—in one great volume. Perfect inexpensive puzzler for clever youngsters. Full solutions. 112pp. 8⅛ x 11.
22951-3 Pa. $5.95

PIANO TUNING, J. Cree Fischer. Clearest, best book for beginner, amateur. Simple repairs, raising dropped notes, tuning by easy method of flattened fifths. No previous skills needed. 4 illustrations. 201pp. 5⅜ x 8½. 23267-0 Pa. $6.95

HINTS TO SINGERS, Lillian Nordica. Selecting the right teacher, developing confidence, overcoming stage fright, and many other important skills receive thoughtful discussion in this indispensible guide, written by a world-famous diva of four decades' experience. 96pp. 5³/₈ x 8¹/₂. 40094-8 Pa. $4.95

THE COMPLETE NONSENSE OF EDWARD LEAR, Edward Lear. All nonsense limericks, zany alphabets, Owl and Pussycat, songs, nonsense botany, etc., illustrated by Lear. Total of 320pp. 5⅜ x 8½. (AVAILABLE IN U.S. ONLY.) 20167-8 Pa. $7.95

VICTORIAN PARLOUR POETRY: An Annotated Anthology, Michael R. Turner. 117 gems by Longfellow, Tennyson, Browning, many lesser-known poets. "The Village Blacksmith," "Curfew Must Not Ring Tonight," "Only a Baby Small," dozens more, often difficult to find elsewhere. Index of poets, titles, first lines. xxiii + 325pp. 5⅜ x 8¼. 27044-0 Pa. $8.95

DUBLINERS, James Joyce. Fifteen stories offer vivid, tightly focused observations of the lives of Dublin's poorer classes. At least one, "The Dead," is considered a masterpiece. Reprinted complete and unabridged from standard edition. 160pp. 5³/₁₆ x 8¼. 26870-5 Pa. $1.00

GREAT WEIRD TALES: 14 Stories by Lovecraft, Blackwood, Machen and Others, S. T. Joshi (ed.). 14 spellbinding tales, including "The Sin Eater," by Fiona McLeod, "The Eye Above the Mantel," by Frank Belknap Long, as well as renowned works by R. H. Barlow, Lord Dunsany, Arthur Machen, W. C. Morrow and eight other masters of the genre. 256pp. 5⅜ x 8½. (Available in U.S. only.) 40436-6 Pa. $8.95

THE BOOK OF THE SACRED MAGIC OF ABRAMELIN THE MAGE, translated by S. MacGregor Mathers. Medieval manuscript of ceremonial magic. Basic document in Aleister Crowley, Golden Dawn groups. 268pp. 5⅜ x 8½. 23211-5 Pa. $9.95

NEW RUSSIAN-ENGLISH AND ENGLISH-RUSSIAN DICTIONARY, M. A. O'Brien. This is a remarkably handy Russian dictionary, containing a surprising amount of information, including over 70,000 entries. 366pp. 4½ x 6⅛. 20208-9 Pa. $10.95

HISTORIC HOMES OF THE AMERICAN PRESIDENTS, Second, Revised Edition, Irvin Haas. A traveler's guide to American Presidential homes, most open to the public, depicting and describing homes occupied by every American President from George Washington to George Bush. With visiting hours, admission charges, travel routes. 175 photographs. Index. 160pp. 8¼ x 11. 26751-2 Pa. $11.95

NEW YORK IN THE FORTIES, Andreas Feininger. 162 brilliant photographs by the well-known photographer, formerly with *Life* magazine. Commuters, shoppers, Times Square at night, much else from city at its peak. Captions by John von Hartz. 181pp. 9¼ x 10¾. 23585-8 Pa. $13.95

INDIAN SIGN LANGUAGE, William Tomkins. Over 525 signs developed by Sioux and other tribes. Written instructions and diagrams. Also 290 pictographs. 111pp. 6⅛ x 9¼. 22029-X Pa. $3.95

CATALOG OF DOVER BOOKS

ANATOMY: A Complete Guide for Artists, Joseph Sheppard. A master of figure drawing shows artists how to render human anatomy convincingly. Over 460 illustrations. 224pp. 8⅜ x 11¼. 27279-6 Pa. $11.95

MEDIEVAL CALLIGRAPHY: Its History and Technique, Marc Drogin. Spirited history, comprehensive instruction manual covers 13 styles (ca. 4th century through 15th). Excellent photographs; directions for duplicating medieval techniques with modern tools. 224pp. 8⅜ x 11¼. 26142-5 Pa. $12.95

DRIED FLOWERS: How to Prepare Them, Sarah Whitlock and Martha Rankin. Complete instructions on how to use silica gel, meal and borax, perlite aggregate, sand and borax, glycerine and water to create attractive permanent flower arrangements. 12 illustrations. 32pp. 5⅜ x 8½. 21802-3 Pa. $1.00

EASY-TO-MAKE BIRD FEEDERS FOR WOODWORKERS, Scott D. Campbell. Detailed, simple-to-use guide for designing, constructing, caring for and using feeders. Text, illustrations for 12 classic and contemporary designs. 96pp. 5⅜ x 8½. 25847-5 Pa. $3.95

SCOTTISH WONDER TALES FROM MYTH AND LEGEND, Donald A. Mackenzie. 16 lively tales tell of giants rumbling down mountainsides, of a magic wand that turns stone pillars into warriors, of gods and goddesses, evil hags, powerful forces and more. 240pp. 5⅜ x 8½. 29677-6 Pa. $6.95

THE HISTORY OF UNDERCLOTHES, C. Willett Cunnington and Phyllis Cunnington. Fascinating, well-documented survey covering six centuries of English undergarments, enhanced with over 100 illustrations: 12th-century laced-up bodice, footed long drawers (1795), 19th-century bustles, 19th-century corsets for men, Victorian "bust improvers," much more. 272pp. 5⅝ x 8¼. 27124-2 Pa. $9.95

ARTS AND CRAFTS FURNITURE: The Complete Brooks Catalog of 1912, Brooks Manufacturing Co. Photos and detailed descriptions of more than 150 now very collectible furniture designs from the Arts and Crafts movement depict davenports, settees, buffets, desks, tables, chairs, bedsteads, dressers and more, all built of solid, quarter-sawed oak. Invaluable for students and enthusiasts of antiques, Americana and the decorative arts. 80pp. 6½ x 9¼. 27471-3 Pa. $8.95

WILBUR AND ORVILLE: A Biography of the Wright Brothers, Fred Howard. Definitive, crisply written study tells the full story of the brothers' lives and work. A vividly written biography, unparalleled in scope and color, that also captures the spirit of an extraordinary era. 560pp. 6⅛ x 9¼. 40297-5 Pa. $17.95

THE ARTS OF THE SAILOR: Knotting, Splicing and Ropework, Hervey Garrett Smith. Indispensable shipboard reference covers tools, basic knots and useful hitches; handsewing and canvas work, more. Over 100 illustrations. Delightful reading for sea lovers. 256pp. 5⅜ x 8½. 26440-8 Pa. $8.95

FRANK LLOYD WRIGHT'S FALLINGWATER: The House and Its History, Second, Revised Edition, Donald Hoffmann. A total revision–both in text and illustrations–of the standard document on Fallingwater, the boldest, most personal architectural statement of Wright's mature years, updated with valuable new material from the recently opened Frank Lloyd Wright Archives. "Fascinating"–*The New York Times*. 116 illustrations. 128pp. 9¼ x 10¾. 27430-6 Pa. $12.95

PHOTOGRAPHIC SKETCHBOOK OF THE CIVIL WAR, Alexander Gardner. 100 photos taken on field during the Civil War. Famous shots of Manassas Harper's Ferry, Lincoln, Richmond, slave pens, etc. 244pp. 10⅝ x 8¼.   22731-6 Pa. $10.95

FIVE ACRES AND INDEPENDENCE, Maurice G. Kains. Great back-to-the-land classic explains basics of self-sufficient farming. The one book to get. 95 illustrations. 397pp. 5⅜ x 8½.   20974-1 Pa. $7.95

SONGS OF EASTERN BIRDS, Dr. Donald J. Borror. Songs and calls of 60 species most common to eastern U.S.: warblers, woodpeckers, flycatchers, thrushes, larks, many more in high-quality recording.   Cassette and manual 99912-2 $9.95

A MODERN HERBAL, Margaret Grieve. Much the fullest, most exact, most useful compilation of herbal material. Gigantic alphabetical encyclopedia, from aconite to zedoary, gives botanical information, medical properties, folklore, economic uses, much else. Indispensable to serious reader. 161 illustrations. 888pp. 6½ x 9¼. 2-vol. set. (Available in U.S. only.)   Vol. I: 22798-7 Pa. $9.95
        Vol. II: 22799-5 Pa. $9.95

HIDDEN TREASURE MAZE BOOK, Dave Phillips. Solve 34 challenging mazes accompanied by heroic tales of adventure. Evil dragons, people-eating plants, blood-thirsty giants, many more dangerous adversaries lurk at every twist and turn. 34 mazes, stories, solutions. 48pp. 8¼ x 11.   24566-7 Pa. $2.95

LETTERS OF W. A. MOZART, Wolfgang A. Mozart. Remarkable letters show bawdy wit, humor, imagination, musical insights, contemporary musical world; includes some letters from Leopold Mozart. 276pp. 5⅜ x 8½.   22859-2 Pa. $7.95

BASIC PRINCIPLES OF CLASSICAL BALLET, Agrippina Vaganova. Great Russian theoretician, teacher explains methods for teaching classical ballet. 118 illustrations. 175pp. 5⅜ x 8½.   22036-2 Pa. $6.95

THE JUMPING FROG, Mark Twain. Revenge edition. The original story of The Celebrated Jumping Frog of Calaveras County, a hapless French translation, and Twain's hilarious "retranslation" from the French. 12 illustrations. 66pp. 5⅜ x 8½.
        22686-7 Pa. $3.95

BEST REMEMBERED POEMS, Martin Gardner (ed.). The 126 poems in this superb collection of 19th- and 20th-century British and American verse range from Shelley's "To a Skylark" to the impassioned "Renascence" of Edna St. Vincent Millay and to Edward Lear's whimsical "The Owl and the Pussycat." 224pp. 5⅜ x 8½.
        27165-X Pa. $5.95

COMPLETE SONNETS, William Shakespeare. Over 150 exquisite poems deal with love, friendship, the tyranny of time, beauty's evanescence, death and other themes in language of remarkable power, precision and beauty. Glossary of archaic terms. 80pp. 5³⁄₁₆ x 8¼.   26686-9 Pa. $1.00

BODIES IN A BOOKSHOP, R. T. Campbell. Challenging mystery of blackmail and murder with ingenious plot and superbly drawn characters. In the best tradition of British suspense fiction. 192pp. 5⅜ x 8½.   24720-1 Pa. $6.95

THE WIT AND HUMOR OF OSCAR WILDE, Alvin Redman (ed.). More than 1,000 ripostes, paradoxes, wisecracks: Work is the curse of the drinking classes; I can resist everything except temptation; etc. 258pp. 5⅜ x 8½.   20602-5 Pa. $6.95

SHAKESPEARE LEXICON AND QUOTATION DICTIONARY, Alexander Schmidt. Full definitions, locations, shades of meaning in every word in plays and poems. More than 50,000 exact quotations. 1,485pp. 6½ x 9¼. 2-vol. set.
Vol. 1: 22726-X Pa. $17.95
Vol. 2: 22727-8 Pa. $17.95

SELECTED POEMS, Emily Dickinson. Over 100 best-known, best-loved poems by one of America's foremost poets, reprinted from authoritative early editions. No comparable edition at this price. Index of first lines. 64pp. 5³⁄₁₆ x 8¼.
26466-1 Pa. $1.00

THE INSIDIOUS DR. FU-MANCHU, Sax Rohmer. The first of the popular mystery series introduces a pair of English detectives to their archnemesis, the diabolical Dr. Fu-Manchu. Flavorful atmosphere, fast-paced action, and colorful characters enliven this classic of the genre. 208pp. 5³⁄₁₆ x 8¼.   29898-1 Pa. $2.00

THE MALLEUS MALEFICARUM OF KRAMER AND SPRENGER, translated by Montague Summers. Full text of most important witchhunter's "bible," used by both Catholics and Protestants. 278pp. 6⅝ x 10.   22802-9 Pa. $12.95

SPANISH STORIES/CUENTOS ESPAÑOLES: A Dual-Language Book, Angel Flores (ed.). Unique format offers 13 great stories in Spanish by Cervantes, Borges, others. Faithful English translations on facing pages. 352pp. 5⅜ x 8½.
25399-6 Pa. $8.95

GARDEN CITY, LONG ISLAND, IN EARLY PHOTOGRAPHS, 1869–1919, Mildred H. Smith. Handsome treasury of 118 vintage pictures, accompanied by carefully researched captions, document the Garden City Hotel fire (1899), the Vanderbilt Cup Race (1908), the first airmail flight departing from the Nassau Boulevard Aerodrome (1911), and much more. 96pp. 8⅞ x 11¾.   40669-5 Pa. $12.95

OLD QUEENS, N.Y., IN EARLY PHOTOGRAPHS, Vincent F. Seyfried and William Asadorian. Over 160 rare photographs of Maspeth, Jamaica, Jackson Heights, and other areas. Vintage views of DeWitt Clinton mansion, 1939 World's Fair and more. Captions. 192pp. 8⅞ x 11.   26358-4 Pa. $12.95

CAPTURED BY THE INDIANS: 15 Firsthand Accounts, 1750-1870, Frederick Drimmer. Astounding true historical accounts of grisly torture, bloody conflicts, relentless pursuits, miraculous escapes and more, by people who lived to tell the tale. 384pp. 5⅜ x 8½.   24901-8 Pa. $8.95

THE WORLD'S GREAT SPEECHES (Fourth Enlarged Edition), Lewis Copeland, Lawrence W. Lamm, and Stephen J. McKenna. Nearly 300 speeches provide public speakers with a wealth of updated quotes and inspiration–from Pericles' funeral oration and William Jennings Bryan's "Cross of Gold Speech" to Malcolm X's powerful words on the Black Revolution and Earl of Spenser's tribute to his sister, Diana, Princess of Wales. 944pp. 5⅜ x 8⅜.   40903-1 Pa. $15.95

THE BOOK OF THE SWORD, Sir Richard F. Burton. Great Victorian scholar/adventurer's eloquent, erudite history of the "queen of weapons"–from prehistory to early Roman Empire. Evolution and development of early swords, variations (sabre, broadsword, cutlass, scimitar, etc.), much more. 336pp. 6⅛ x 9¼.
25434-8 Pa. $9.95

AUTOBIOGRAPHY: The Story of My Experiments with Truth, Mohandas K. Gandhi. Boyhood, legal studies, purification, the growth of the Satyagraha (nonviolent protest) movement. Critical, inspiring work of the man responsible for the freedom of India. 480pp. 5⅜ x 8½. (Available in U.S. only.) 24593-4 Pa. $8.95

CELTIC MYTHS AND LEGENDS, T. W. Rolleston. Masterful retelling of Irish and Welsh stories and tales. Cuchulain, King Arthur, Deirdre, the Grail, many more. First paperback edition. 58 full-page illustrations. 512pp. 5⅜ x 8½. 26507-2 Pa. $9.95

THE PRINCIPLES OF PSYCHOLOGY, William James. Famous long course complete, unabridged. Stream of thought, time perception, memory, experimental methods; great work decades ahead of its time. 94 figures. 1,391pp. 5⅜ x 8½. 2-vol. set.
Vol. I: 20381-6 Pa. $14.95
Vol. II: 20382-4 Pa. $14.95

THE WORLD AS WILL AND REPRESENTATION, Arthur Schopenhauer. Definitive English translation of Schopenhauer's life work, correcting more than 1,000 errors, omissions in earlier translations. Translated by E. F. J. Payne. Total of 1,269pp. 5⅜ x 8½. 2-vol. set.
Vol. 1: 21761-2 Pa. $12.95
Vol. 2: 21762-0 Pa. $12.95

MAGIC AND MYSTERY IN TIBET, Madame Alexandra David-Neel. Experiences among lamas, magicians, sages, sorcerers, Bonpa wizards. A true psychic discovery. 32 illustrations. 321pp. 5⅜ x 8½. (Available in U.S. only.) 22682-4 Pa. $9.95

THE EGYPTIAN BOOK OF THE DEAD, E. A. Wallis Budge. Complete reproduction of Ani's papyrus, finest ever found. Full hieroglyphic text, interlinear transliteration, word-for-word translation, smooth translation. 533pp. 6½ x 9¼.
21866-X Pa. $12.95

MATHEMATICS FOR THE NONMATHEMATICIAN, Morris Kline. Detailed, college-level treatment of mathematics in cultural and historical context, with numerous exercises. Recommended Reading Lists. Tables. Numerous figures. 641pp. 5⅜ x 8½.
24823-2 Pa. $11.95

PROBABILISTIC METHODS IN THE THEORY OF STRUCTURES, Isaac Elishakoff. Well-written introduction covers the elements of the theory of probability from two or more random variables, the reliability of such multivariable structures, the theory of random function, Monte Carlo methods of treating problems incapable of exact solution, and more. Examples. 502pp. 5³/₈ x 8¹/₂. 40691-1 Pa. $16.95

THE RIME OF THE ANCIENT MARINER, Gustave Doré, S. T. Coleridge. Doré's finest work; 34 plates capture moods, subtleties of poem. Flawless full-size reproductions printed on facing pages with authoritative text of poem. "Beautiful. Simply beautiful."–*Publisher's Weekly.* 77pp. 9¼ x 12. 22305-1 Pa. $7.95

NORTH AMERICAN INDIAN DESIGNS FOR ARTISTS AND CRAFTSPEOPLE, Eva Wilson. Over 360 authentic copyright-free designs adapted from Navajo blankets, Hopi pottery, Sioux buffalo hides, more. Geometrics, symbolic figures, plant and animal motifs, etc. 128pp. 8⅜ x 11. (Not for sale in the United Kingdom.) 25341-4 Pa. $9.95

SCULPTURE: Principles and Practice, Louis Slobodkin. Step-by-step approach to clay, plaster, metals, stone; classical and modern. 253 drawings, photos. 255pp. 8⅛ x 11.
22960-2 Pa. $11.95

CATALOG OF DOVER BOOKS

THE INFLUENCE OF SEA POWER UPON HISTORY, 1660–1783, A. T. Mahan. Influential classic of naval history and tactics still used as text in war colleges. First paperback edition. 4 maps. 24 battle plans. 640pp. 5⅜ x 8½. 25509-3 Pa. $14.95

THE STORY OF THE TITANIC AS TOLD BY ITS SURVIVORS, Jack Winocour (ed.). What it was really like. Panic, despair, shocking inefficiency, and a little heroism. More thrilling than any fictional account. 26 illustrations. 320pp. 5⅜ x 8½. 20610-6 Pa. $8.95

FAIRY AND FOLK TALES OF THE IRISH PEASANTRY, William Butler Yeats (ed.). Treasury of 64 tales from the twilight world of Celtic myth and legend: "The Soul Cages," "The Kildare Pooka," "King O'Toole and his Goose," many more. Introduction and Notes by W. B. Yeats. 352pp. 5⅜ x 8½. 26941-8 Pa. $8.95

BUDDHIST MAHAYANA TEXTS, E. B. Cowell and others (eds.). Superb, accurate translations of basic documents in Mahayana Buddhism, highly important in history of religions. The Buddha-karita of Asvaghosha, Larger Sukhavativyuha, more. 448pp. 5⅜ x 8½. 25552-2 Pa. $12.95

ONE TWO THREE . . . INFINITY: Facts and Speculations of Science, George Gamow. Great physicist's fascinating, readable overview of contemporary science: number theory, relativity, fourth dimension, entropy, genes, atomic structure, much more. 128 illustrations. Index. 352pp. 5⅜ x 8½. 25664-2 Pa. $9.95

EXPERIMENTATION AND MEASUREMENT, W. J. Youden. Introductory manual explains laws of measurement in simple terms and offers tips for achieving accuracy and minimizing errors. Mathematics of measurement, use of instruments, experimenting with machines. 1994 edition. Foreword. Preface. Introduction. Epilogue. Selected Readings. Glossary. Index. Tables and figures. 128pp. 5⅜ x 8½. 40451-X Pa. $6.95

DALÍ ON MODERN ART: The Cuckolds of Antiquated Modern Art, Salvador Dalí. Influential painter skewers modern art and its practitioners. Outrageous evaluations of Picasso, Cézanne, Turner, more. 15 renderings of paintings discussed. 44 calligraphic decorations by Dalí. 96pp. 5⅜ x 8½. (Available in U.S. only.) 29220-7 Pa. $5.95

ANTIQUE PLAYING CARDS: A Pictorial History, Henry René D'Allemagne. Over 900 elaborate, decorative images from rare playing cards (14th–20th centuries): Bacchus, death, dancing dogs, hunting scenes, royal coats of arms, players cheating, much more. 96pp. 9¼ x 12¼. 29265-7 Pa. $12.95

MAKING FURNITURE MASTERPIECES: 30 Projects with Measured Drawings, Franklin H. Gottshall. Step-by-step instructions, illustrations for constructing handsome, useful pieces, among them a Sheraton desk, Chippendale chair, Spanish desk, Queen Anne table and a William and Mary dressing mirror. 224pp. 8⅛ x 11¼. 29338-6 Pa. $13.95

THE FOSSIL BOOK: A Record of Prehistoric Life, Patricia V. Rich et al. Profusely illustrated definitive guide covers everything from single-celled organisms and dinosaurs to birds and mammals and the interplay between climate and man. Over 1,500 illustrations. 760pp. 7½ x 10⅛. 29371-8 Pa. $29.95

Prices subject to change without notice.

Available at your book dealer or write for free catalog to Dept. GI, Dover Publications, Inc., 31 East 2nd St., Mineola, N.Y. 11501. Dover publishes more than 500 books each year on science, elementary and advanced mathematics, biology, music, art, literary history, social sciences and other areas.